The Knights Templar Chronology

Tracking History's Most Intriguing Monks

By

George Smart

Foreword by Niven Sinclair

1663 Liberty Drive, Suite 200
Bloomington, Indiana 47403
(800) 839-8640
www.AuthorHouse.com

© 2005 George Smart. All Rights Reserved.

No part of this book may be reproduced, stored in a retrieval system, or transmitted by any means without the written permission of the author.

First published by AuthorHouse 12/20/04

ISBN: 1-4184-9890-4 (e)
ISBN: 1-4184-9889-0 (sc)

Library of Congress Control Number: 2004097018

Printed in the United States of America
Bloomington, Indiana

This book is printed on acid-free paper.

Acclaim for <u>The Knights Templar Chronology</u>

"George's book draws our attention to an Order which found the need to build bridges of trust and faith rather than walls of suspicion and fear. Let us hope it finds its way into the White House library and into every other library in the land. We would do well to look for the path of peace before Armageddon becomes the inevitable consequence of Man's insanity."

-- from the Foreword by **Niven Sinclair**, legendary Knights Templar researcher and author of <u>Beyond the Shadow of a Doubt</u>

"I wish I had had this sort of reference work when I was writing <u>The Age of Heretics</u>. <u>The Knights Templar Chronology</u> profiles an influential and significant core group, a group whose impact spanned centuries. It is also an impassioned manifesto, which lets people struggling against the subtle status quo know: You are not alone."

-- **Art Kleiner,** author of <u>The Age of Heretics</u> and <u>The Fifth Discipline Fieldbook</u>

"Eight years of dedication...a labour of love...it has been an honour to be at the side of George Smart as he painstakingly researched, traveled and thought this project through to fruition."

-- **Brother R.T. (Dick) James,** Army & Navy Lodge No. 306, Hampton, Virginia; Cass Lodge No. 243, Coon Rapids, Minnesota

"The Knights Templar Chronology, along with its maps, is the most complete Chronology that I have seen. It should be a must for any reference Librarian or any student of the Middle Ages."

-- Harry B. Lyon, PM, MPS, Asst. Librarian, The George Washington Masonic National Memorial, Washington, DC

Table of Contents

Foreword ix

From the Author.. xiii

Map 1A. France... xix

Map 1B. France before the Crusades. Adapted <u>from French Civilization</u> by Albert Leon Guerard, Houghton Mifflin, 1921 edition. xx

Map 2. Middle East... xxi

Map 3. Israel and the Holy Land xxii

Map 4. Edinburgh, Scotland. xxiii

Map 5. Europe. xxiv

Map 6. Spain. xxv

Map 7. Northeast North America. xxvi

Chapter One: Prelude to War 1

Chapter Two: The First Crusade 6

Chapter Three: Beginnings 14

Chapter Four: Warriors, Monks, Bankers, Statesmen............ 26

Chapter Five: Downfall 65

Bibliography 81

Foreword

What is it about the Knights Templar which has attracted so much interest and which still has a magical aura even after nearly a millennium? Why did they attract men from noble families to their ranks? Why did Kings and others donate property to the Order? Why did the Pope decree that the Order would only be answerable to him? And why, in 1307, were the most specious of pretexts used by another Pope to ban the Knights? There are whole forests of question marks that need to be answered.

There have been hundreds of books attempting to capture the magic and mystery surrounding the most amazing Order in history - an Order which transcended national boundaries and which was respected and feared by friend and foe alike.

We think of the Knights as the warriors of Christ but they were much more than that. True, they fought with valour but they also introduced the equivalent of the credit card that allowed people to use the same currency from the Holy Land to Scotland and everywhere in between. There is nothing new about the idea of a common currency for Europe. The Templars saw the need as it facilitated travel and trade. We see evidence of their financial activities from the rock churches of Ethiopia to their presence in Mexico as early as 1241 A.D.

What motivated them? It is said they left no written history but their history is in their deeds. In any event, true history is not always in the written word. It is:

-- in the faces of the people we meet
-- in the language we speak
-- in our customs, traditions and superstitions
-- in our genes which travel further than the person who first introduced them
-- in the ground under our feet
-- in evidence of cultural diffusion between Continents

George Smart has taken on the task of writing <u>The Knights Templar Chronology</u> to give all future researchers a framework on which to build -- but he has done more than that. In this absorbing work, he has whetted our appetite for even more information about the poor warrior monks who, paradoxically, belonged to the richest Order in Christendom. Nevertheless, they understood the need for a rapprochement with Islam - a rapprochement which is just as necessary today as it was in their era. Equally, there is a need to return to the ideals of chivalry and fraternity which motivated the Templars and their military foe, the great Arab leader, Saladin. A classic example of chivalry happened late in the 12th century. Upon seeing the horse of King Richard the Lionheart had been shot beneath him, Saladin sent the King a fresh horse.

Courage and chivalry are not the preserve of any one nation or of any one people. These qualities are evidenced whenever men of honour meet on the battlefield or at the United Nations. In truth, these qualities have been in short supply in recent years as positions become increasingly polarised between war and anti-war lobbies.

We need men today of the calibre and the wisdom of the Templars. It may be that the resurgence of interest in the Order reflects a growing realisation that Mankind has strayed, with such catastrophic results, from the path of learning and understanding on to the narrow path of fear and hatred of anything and everything that is different.

In reality, regardless of our colour or creed, we are all at one with each other in our primitive mortal needs. That is the lesson which we have to learn. That was the lesson which the Templars learned from their years of struggle in the Middle East. It is a lesson which we would do well to take on board before there is even more needless suffering in this tormented and troubled World.

George's book draws our attention to an Order that found the need to build bridges of trust and faith rather than walls of suspicion and fear. Let us hope it finds its way into the White House library and into every other library in the land. We would do well to look for the path of peace before Armageddon becomes the inevitable consequence of Man's insanity.

Niven Sinclair

From the Author

As few things captivate the human mind and imagination as a story unfinished, the Knights Templars' purpose, organization, secret rituals, achievements, influence, and disappearance have become one of the most persistent and enduring mysteries in history.

These warrior-monks have been the subject of countless books over the years but the public has been largely ignorant of their exploits until recently. With the runaway success of the Da Vinci Code, a novel by Dan Brown prominently featuring Templar History, more and more people are curious about this most intriguing group of knights. But while Dan Brown has certainly been the most financially successful author (Forbes estimates Da Vinci Code books, spin-offs, and movie will gross over a billion dollars in sales), he is not the first. Michael Baigent, Richard Leigh, and Henry Lincoln pioneered this era's wave of Templar interest with their 1982 bestseller Holy Blood Holy Grail and its sequels The Messianic Legacy and Temple and the Lodge.

Brown draws heavily from the extensive research of Baigent, Lincoln, and Leigh (as have many authors since, including this one) to weave an explosively controversial story, an essential contradiction to the orthodox Christian view of Jesus and Mary Magdalene. Far from the simplistic view of them as God/Savior and reformed prostitute wrapped in politics between the Jews and the Romans, Brown suggests that during the 12th century the Knights Templar discovered and became guardians of the true story of Jesus -- that he and his wealthy, educated benefactor Mary Magdalene fell in love, were married before the crucifixion, and had children who carry a bloodline forward to today.

As religion is a matter of faith, and faith is based on non-reason, it matters little to devout Christians what research Brown, Baigent, Leigh, Lincoln, or any contemporary authors put forth. According to the faithful, we have no record of his life other than the Bible and that account is unfalteringly true. Jesus is God and above and beyond any sort of earthly procreation. Fundamentalists reject any other source than the Bible or works by adherents of that orthodox story. Other accounts, including the Nag Hammadi scrolls, are considered not just false, but completely without credibility. Jesus is God, period, and the whole marriage/children thing with Mary Magdalene is impossible, sacrilegious, and perhaps subversive.

Without question Jesus is worthy of our reverence. Nearly all religions speak of Jesus for his wisdom, for his kindness, for his tolerance, for his forgiveness, for his teachings, for his courage, and for his love of humanity, among many, many other wonderful qualities. Even the *Qur'an*, the holy book of Islam, speaks of Jesus in exceptionally admiring terms.

What is worthy of closer inspection are the facts surrounding his life. More people are questioning the accepted version of Jesus and Mary Magdalene. Biblical scholars such as the Jesus Seminar exhaustively analyzed the Bible in the 1990's to establish which parts are mostly likely true and which parts, as happens to any book, have been edited, altered, enhanced, or destroyed for various reasons over hundreds of years. Other researchers pursue the bloodline theory and a succession of guardians of original scrolls proving it. No one, regardless of their beliefs on the facts of his life, questions the character of Jesus. Finding a less miraculous, more human story only enhances Jesus' stature as one of civilization's greatest men.

Between the lifetime of Jesus and the beginning of the Knights Templar, the Western world goes through the Dark Ages, a largely self-imposed isolation from science, from learning, and from other cultures, especially in the East and Far East. Prohibitions on Catholic pilgrimages to Jerusalem cause the Pope to break this cultural exile and declare a Holy war on Islam which is successful. Christianity retakes Jerusalem and establishes rule. About 15 years later, Knights Templar surface in France in the Middle Ages as a monastic order established under the guidance of history's most famous monk, Saint Bernard. Conventional historians such as Barber, Burman, Partner, and Sanello cite the Templars' primary purpose as protection of Catholics on pilgrimages from Europe to Jerusalem. However, it makes no sense that this was their *real* function. For nine years there were just nine guys and even as fierce knight/warrior/monks, nine guys simply cannot protect the hundreds of pilgrims along hundreds of miles to Jerusalem. Whatever they were doing, they were doing it without growing in numbers as there is no evidence Templars recruited during the first nine years.

The treatment of these nine monks was also far beyond normal. When they first arrived in Jerusalem, King Bauduoin II accorded them extensive property and support. Common monks, bound to vows of poverty, did not normally receive this kind of attention. It has one wonder why the Templars were really in Jerusalem. Since they were not protecting any pilgrims, what was their actual purpose? So far, the most likely explanation is archeological, that they were digging for something under the Temple Mount – and found it. Various theories include:

- Treasure taken from the Jews or others by the Romans;
- A cache of original scrolls (including Gospels that did not make the <u>Bible's</u> final edition) by or about Jesus, Mary Magdalene, and the apostles;
- The body or other parts of Jesus, preserved in some form since the crucifixion;
- The head of John the Baptist;
- Relics of Jesus, such as the cross upon which he was crucified, his burial shroud, and, the crown of thorns;
- The body of Alexander the Great, preserved since its disappearance after his death;
- Scrolls from the Library of Alexandria saved from various attacks;
- Early Hebrew sacred literature possibly contained in the fabled Ark of the Covenant.

Over the ensuing 180 years, the Templars experienced unprecedented growth in wealth, power, influence, and property across England, the Continent, and the Middle East. Various Popes granted the Order immunity from all taxes and accountability to other rulers. With circular preceptories (like branch offices), their work as bankers, statesmen, and military advisors/trainers exerted control over warehousing, commerce, politics, and even Papal appointments. Their Paris preceptory was the central bank of Europe. They invented the check and the prototype of the banking system we use today. Templars were among the first Westerners to use a magnetic compass. They were arrogant (and powerful) enough to even defy the Papacy at times. Contrary to Papal policy, the Templars established good relationships with the "infidels" (Muslims and Jews) and learned their advancements in science, cartography, and philosophy. Templars especially immersed themselves in Muslim knowledge, for example, adopting the Atbash cipher for coded communication. Their acceptance of other religions extended beyond secular interests to the theological as well. According to Andrew Sinclair's <u>The Sword and the Grail</u>, the Knights Templar believed in "the One God, the Architect of the World, in whom the members of all religions, Christian and Muslim and Jew, might believe." This makes them one of the most spiritually progressive groups of their time -- perhaps of all time.

Their influence with various Popes and rulers, and the inevitable arrogance that comes with immense power, ultimately led to their downfall at the hands of a very greedy King of France. But during their heyday, everyone wanted to be a Templar.

To better understand their story, this chronology begins with the events leading to the first crusade, a Catholic response to Seljuk Turks sealing off the holy city of Jerusalem and threatening the West. Later you'll meet the nine brave men who were there in the beginning, the nine original Templars:

- Hugues de Payns, a vassal of Count Hugues de Champagne
- André de Montbard, also a vassal of Count Hugues de Champagne, and Bernard de Fontaine (Saint Bernard's) uncle
- Godfroi de Saint Omer (a.k.a. Geoffroi de St. Omer, Bisol de St. Omer)

- Payen de Montdidier from the ruling house of Flanders (a.k.a. Payen de Montdesir, Nivard de Montdidier)
- Archambaud de Saint-Agnan from the ruling house of Flanders (a.k.a. Archambaud de St-Amand)
- Jacques de Rossal (a.k.a. Raffle)
- Godfroi
- Godfroi de Bisor (a.k.a. Geoffroi Bisol)
- André de Gondemare

Whether the Templars were simply monks carrying out the work of the Church or guardians of secret bloodline – or both -- their tale has captured imaginations for centuries. I wrote this book to provide current and future Templar detectives the essential timeline to put clues in order.

Years of researching, traveling, and writing could not have happened without great supporters. Foremost, I thank Niven Sinclair, whose tireless research, sponsorship, devotion, and development of Templar history is unmatched in this century. Beyond his generosity in writing the Foreword, Niven connected me to essential books, contacts, and points of view inaccessible without his assistance. Paul Bessel and Harry Lyon introduced me to Masonry and their incredible labor of love, the restoration of the George Washington Masonic National Memorial Library in Washington, DC. This is truly a special place, now viewable only by appointment. Dick James, Judith Fisken, Peter Moss, Pierre Meste, and Jennifer Sumner helped with research and supplied a steady stream of encouragement and ideas. Stephen Dafoe of www.templarhistory.com graciously provided a graphic used for the cover and at the bottom of each page. My parents George and Ann Smart gave endless love and support. Chuck Grubb edited along with Cindy and Rachel Stratton, Bonnie Auslander, Anne Murray, Bonnie Favorite, Liz Guzynski, Christine Testolini, and my beloved Eleanor Stell.

The Knights Templar Chronology is dedicated to expanding knowledge on history's most intriguing monks and creating opportunities and funding for more direct, archeological research to discover their legacy.

George Smart
www.georgesmart.net

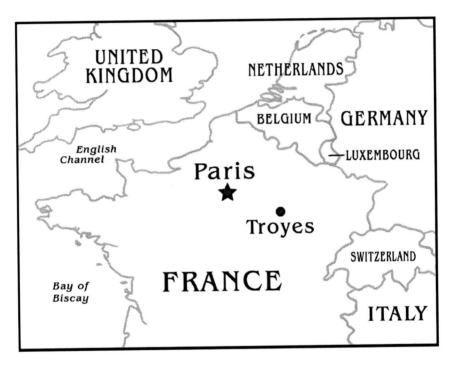

Map 1A. France.

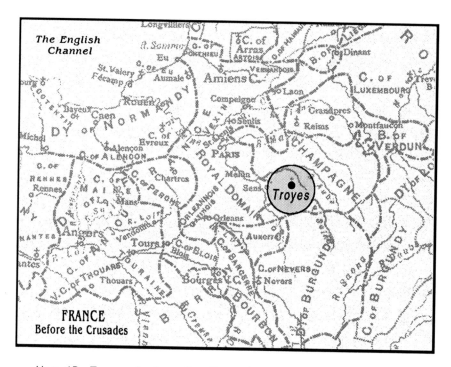

Map 1B. France before the Crusades. Adapted <u>from French Civilization</u> by Albert Leon Guerard, Houghton Mifflin, 1921 edition.

Map 2. Middle East.

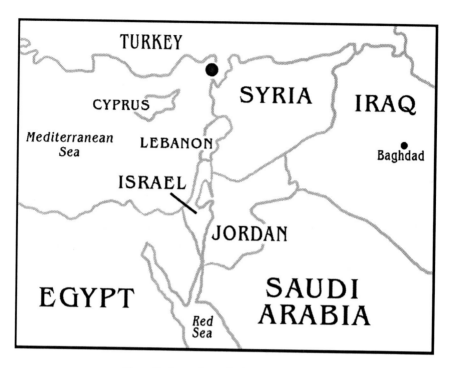

Map 3. Israel and the Holy Land

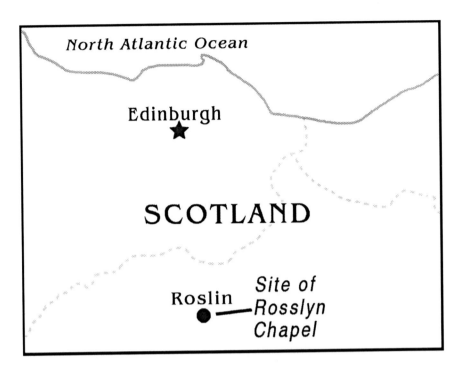

Map 4. Edinburgh, Scotland.

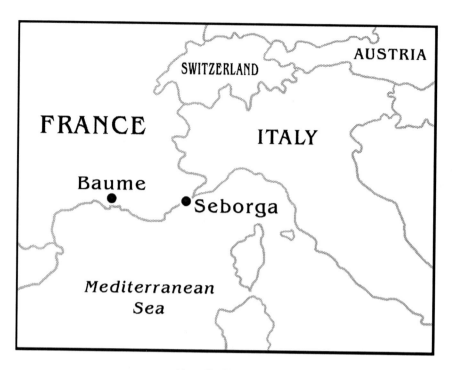

Map 5. Europe.

Map 6. Spain.

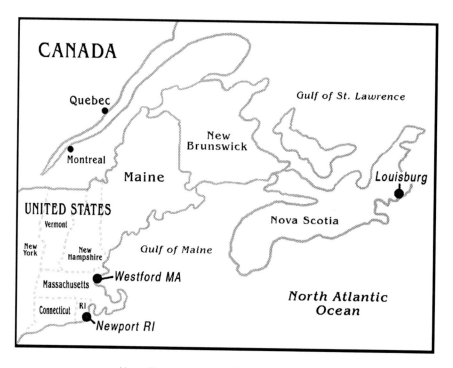

Map 7. Northeast North America.

Chapter One:
Prelude to War

As the world slowly pulls out of the Dark Ages, factions largely divided by religious differences carve up Europe. Scholars study manuscripts rescued from various military purges and book-burnings, looking for clues to a closer connection with God, treasure, or religious artifacts. Meanwhile power changes hands in the Middle East, and the stage is set for a Christian war known as the crusade.

| 1065 | Rabbi Shlomo Yitzhaki (a.k.a. Rashi, 1040-1105), Jewish expert on the Bible and the Talmud, founds a school of Kabbala and other esoteric subjects in the Court of Champagne at Troyes, long a haven for Jews and other non-Catholics fleeing persecution. The school lasts over 200 years. As a Jew and a scholar, he was protected from persecution by various Counts in exchange for his exceptional translation abilities, including translating Hebrew into French. Due to his intellect, years of study, and access to ancient texts, Rashi was the foremost expert on the Holy Land in his day. A winemaker by trade, Rashi taught his daughters to read and write in an age when educating women was rare. Rashi's commentary became the world's first dated book printed in Hebrew and was widely distributed among Jewish scholars.

See Maps 1a. and 1b.

During Rashi's lifetime, Jewish religious scholars believed the Ark of the Covenant and other religious treasure are buried beneath the *Shetiyyah* (foundation stone) of the Temple Mount in Jerusalem prior to the Babylonian invasion of 587 BC.

A large group of Catholic nobles arrive on a pilgrimage to Jerusalem -- including the Count of Barcelona, the Count of Luxemburg, the Count of Flanders, Bringer-Raymond of Barcelona, William IV de Toulouse, and four German bishops.

1066 Alp Arslän (1029-1072), second Sultan of the Seljuk Turks, unsuccessfully attacks Byzantine Christians who centuries earlier separated from the Catholic Church based in Rome. The Roman Pope expresses support for the victims but does not commit any military resources to help them.

1070	Birth of future Templar Hugues de Payns in the town of Payns, 10 km from Troyes in France.
	Peter the Hermit serves as a tutor to the young Godfroi de Bouillon (born 1060) as a minor noble connected to Eustace de Boulogne, Godfroi's father. He later becomes a monk at Orval, home to a mysterious order from Calabria in northern Italy who avidly researched the bloodline of the Godfroi's family.
1071	On August 19, Seljuk Turks under Sultan Alp Arslän kidnap and defeat Byzantine Christian Emperor Romanus IV. Later that fall, Sultan Alp Arslän's forces take control of Jerusalem and begin plans for taking Constantinople. See Maps 2 and 3.
1072	Sultan Alp Arslän's son, third Sultan Jalal al-Din Malikshah (1055-1092), prohibits European Catholics from making pilgrimages to Jerusalem, a ban which enrages Pope Alexander II.
1073	Pope Gregory VII (1020-1085) takes office and institutes Catholic reforms against simony, clerical marriage, and lay investiture, a process transferring Abbeys and other Church properties to secular powers. He issues *Dictatus papae*, an edict which proclaims the supremacy of the Pope over all others, starting a long running conflict with Holy Roman Emperor Henry IV (1050-1108).
1074	Pope Gregory VII calls for a crusade against the Seljuk Turks for closing off Jerusalem but, because of continuing conflicts with Holy Roman Emperor Henry IV, fails to get enough support to organize a military response.
1076	During the Synod at Worms, in a dispute over lay investiture, Holy Roman Emperor Henry IV deposes Pope Gregory VII who in turn excommunicates him. They reconcile in 1077 but split again three years later.

1079 Castrum Sepulchri (later the principality of Seborga) becomes a principality of the Holy Roman Empire under Emperor Henry IV. See Map 5.

1080 Sufi Al-Hasan ibn al-Sabbah (a.k.a., the Old Man of the Mountain, 1034-1124) starts the Order of the Devoted of Assassins, an Ismaili sect of Islam. Based at the fortress of Alamut in Persia, the Assassins successfully use strategic murder (assassination, names after them) to gain power, land, and wealth.

1084 Holy Roman Emperor Henry IV conquers Rome and replaces Pope Gregory VII with his own man, Clement III, in Rome.

1085 Seljuk Turks capture Antioch, expelling the Byzantine Christians from Syria.

King Alfonso VI of Castille (1030-1109) captures Toledo in Spain from the Moors.

Catholic troops force the Jewish population in Spain into France, despite the fact Jews in Spain had lived peacefully with their Muslim rulers for centuries,

1086 Berber Muslim leader Yusuf ibn Tashfin of the al-Morovids defeats King Alfonso VI of Castille and retakes Spain for the Moors.

1087 Death of Pope Gregory VII.

1088   Urban II (1042-1099) becomes Pope but is kept from Rome by Holy Roman Emperor Henry IV and his appointee, Clement III.

Peter the Hermit (1050-1115) travels from Jerusalem to meet Pope Urban II. He brings an impassioned plea from Simeon, the Patriarch of Jerusalem, for aid and an offer of reconciliation between the Eastern and Western churches.

Death of Berengar de Tours (born 1000), a Catholic theologian who believes that while Jesus is present spiritually at the time of communion, literal transformation of wine into blood defies common sense.

1089   At the Council of Melfi, Pope Urban II and Byzantine Emperor Alexius Comnenus (1048-1118) lift their excommunications of each other.

1091   The Seljuk Turks establish a capital at Baghdad.

1092   After the death of Muslim Sultan Malikshah, the Seljuk Turk empire breaks up into smaller sultanates plus independent principalities of the Atabegs in Syria, upper Mesopotamia and Azarbaijan.

1093   French King Philippe grants the young Count Hugues de Champagne (1077-1126) his daughter Constance in marriage.

1094   Pope Urban II returns to Rome.

Chapter Two:
The First Crusade

If in 1095 there was a Catholic most-wanted list, Muslims would be at the very top. Muslims accept and acknowledge the wisdom of Jesus but they refuse to recognize him as God -- or the Papacy as the ultimate earthly authority from God. Overall, Muslims tolerate other faiths, much more so than Christians. In Muslim lands, Jews, Catholics, Muslims, Greeks, and many other faiths live in relative peace. However, Muslim rulers are not without ambition, and attacks on Byzantine Christian territory are common. It is not until Muslims restrict Europeans from making pilgrimages to Jerusalem that Catholics get mad - and murderous. Catholic forces, ignoring their most basic tenets ('Thou shalt not kill' comes to mind), become exceptionally eager to kill those outside Christianity, even their own Byzantine brethren. The massacres during the First Crusade are among the most brutal in history and establish a pattern of violence throughout the Holy Land for centuries.

1095 In the spring, Byzantine Emperor Alexius Comnenus sends legates from Constantinople to the Pope Urban II's Council of Piacenza requesting military help against the Seljuk Turks.

On November 27, Pope Urban II calls for the First Crusade at the Council of Clermont-Ferrand to take back the Holy Land. He stays in France for the next year to help organize troops and supplies.

1096 Having sold his castle and all his estates, Duke of Lower Lorraine, Godfroi de Bouillon (1061-1100) departs France as commander of the First Crusade. Other crusaders include:

- His brother Baudouin of Boulougne (dies 1118)
- His brother Eustace IV (1059-1125)
- His cousin Baudouin du Bourg
- Marcus Bohemond I of Tarento, Norman Prince of Sicily
- Marcus Bohemond's nephew Tancred the Norman
- Bishop Adhemar of Le Puy, Papal Legate (dies 1098), who will carry the "Holy Lance" after its "discovery" in Antioch
- Count of Toulouse and St. Gilles Raimond IV
- Count of Vermandois Hugh the Great, brother of the French King of Northern and Central France
- Baron Henri de Saint Clair (1058-1110), son of William Saint Clair and Dorothy Dunbar
- Duke of Normandy Robert, eldest son of William the Conqueror
- Robert of Normandy's sister Adele
- Adele's husband Etienne de Blois (a.k.a. Stephen of Blois), son of Count Thibaud I de Champagne and half-brother to Count Hugues de Champagne)
- Etienne de Blois's cousin Robert II, Count of Flanders
- Hugues de Payns (February 9, 1070 to 1136)

In March, Pope Urban II sends a unit of commoners (the People's Crusade) under the command of Peter the Hermit and knight Walter Sans-Avoir (a.k.a. Walter the Penniless). While in Nicea, Sultan Kali Arslän kills Walter but Peter escapes and rejoins de Bouillon's forces near Nicomedia the next year.

According to Andrew Sinclair in <u>The Sword and The Grail</u>, all nine future Templars are involved with de Bouillon on the First Crusade.

1097 The First Crusade reaches Constantinople, conquers Nicea, and moves to besiege Antioch from October through the following June.

1098 In October, Pope Urban II convenes the Council of Bari in a futile attempt to reconcile Roman and Byzantine Christians.

In November, the First Crusade captures Edessa.

Only about one-third of the knights who left Europe for the First Crusade are still alive at this point.

1099 On July 15, Godfroi de Bouillon captures Jerusalem. In over a week of incredible carnage, crusaders kill more than seventy thousand people. They kill Muslims in the al-Aqsa Mosque. They burn Jews inside synagogues. They destroy the monuments of saints, the mosque of Umar and the tomb of Abraham. Only Count Raimond de Toulouse shows any small sign of mercy. At the Tower of David, he allows some citizens to buy their freedom and leave the city unharmed.

On July 29, Paschal II assumes the Papacy when Urban II dies.

In August at Ascalon, de Bouillon defeats Egyptian forces moving towards Jerusalem. Peter the Hermit is administrator of Jerusalem while de Bouillon is out of town.

Hugues de Payns returns to Europe to become a vassal for Count Hugues de Champagne, one of the wealthiest lords in Europe.

A secret conclave offers Count Raimond de Toulouse the title of King of Jerusalem but he refuses. They offer the title next to de Bouillon, who declines for religious reasons (no one should be King other than Jesus, in his opinion) and instead chooses the title of Defender of the Holy Sepulchre. De Bouillon builds the Church of the Holy Sepulchre on this famous site where Jesus was buried after his crucifixion and establishes the Sacred and Military Order of the Holy Sepulchre of Jerusalem to protect it. He converts the al-Aqsa Mosque to a royal palace.

According to Holy Blood, Holy Grail, de Bouillon and other family members, all descendants of Jesus, start the Prieuré de Sion (a.k.a. Prieuré de Sion). De Bouillon builds the impressive Abbey of Notre Dame du Mont de Sion as the organization's headquarters. Until 1118 the Prieuré de Sion and the Templars share the same Grand Master.

1100   On July 18 de Bouillon dies and crusaders bury him in the Church of the Holy Sepulchre. On December 11, his brother Count Baudouin of Edessa becomes King of Jerusalem.

Peter the Hermit returns to Europe in 1100 and founds the monastery of Neufmoutier in Flanders on land provided by de Bouillon's family.

1101   Hugues de Payns marries Frenchwoman Catherine de Saint Clair (niece of fellow crusader Baron Henri de Saint Clair).

In mid-summer, Sultan Kilij Arslän kills thousands of colonists traveling to Jerusalem from Lombardy led by Count Raimond de Toulouse. Raimond narrowly escapes.

In August, fifteen thousand colonists led by the Count of Nevers are killed in Nicea by Sultan Kilij Arslän. The Count and a few others escape to Antioch.

In September, William IX of Aquitaine and Welf IV Duke of Bavaria take thousands more colonists to the Jerusalem, where Arslän's troops have poisoned or filled wells. Badly dehydrated, the colonists finally arrive at a river where Arslän's archers kill almost everyone.

1102   In March, Tancred the Norman is named Prince of Antioch and ravages Muslim neighborhoods.

In April, Count Raimond de Toulouse and his last 300 knights attack Arslän at Tripoli and kill 7000.

1103   Count Raimond de Toulouse begins a siege of Tripoli.

Tughtekin, Governor of Damascus, frees Marcus Bohemond I of Tarento for a ransom which Bohemond recoups by pillaging villages before returning to Europe.

King Baudouin I attacks Haifa and Acre.

1104   According to Dr. Johannes Fiebag and Peter Fiebag in <u>The Eternity Machine</u>, Count Hugues de Champagne funds research using Cistercian monks at Citeaux and Rashi scholars from Troyes to translate ancient Hebrew texts taken from Toledo in search of treasure and artifacts. Perhaps, even the Holy Grail. The Fiebags believe the Grail is a machine from an advanced (meaning not of this world) culture that produced an algae-culture "manna" from water and radiation from using a nuclear-powered light-source.

At the Council of Troyes, Count Hugues de Champagne gives land to several religious groups including the Cistercians of Molesmes.

According to <u>Holy Blood, Holy Grail,</u> Count Hugues de Champagne meets in Molesmes with nobles from the esteemed families of Chaumont (of Gisors), Brienne, and Joinville -- including the liege lord of Andre de Montbard, future Templar and Tibaud I de Payns (1055-1130), Lord of Gisors and cousin to Templar Hugues de Payns.

After getting his marriage to Constance de France annulled for lack of an heir, Count Hugues de Champagne and Hugues de Payns leave from Molesmes for their first visit to the Temple Mount in Jerusalem.

Crusaders take Acre and destroy the city and its population.

At the Battle of Harrân, Seljuk Turks move against Edessa capturing Baudouin of Edessa and his cousin Jocelin de Courtenay on May 7.

1105   On February 28, Count Raimond de Toulouse dies waiting out the siege of Tripoli.

Henry V (1081-1125) forces his father, Holy Roman Emperor Henry IV, to abdicate.

Hugh of St. Omer, Lord of Tiberias, builds the Castel Toron in Tyre.

1106   On September 28, King Henry I of England defeats his brother Robert at the Battle of Tinchebrai, reuniting England and the Normandy area in France.

With funding from Count Hugues de Champagne, a new church is consecrated at Citeaux.

| 1108 | Hugues de Payns and Count Hugues de Champagne return from Jerusalem. The meet in Châtillon-sur-Seine with the same families of Chaumont, Nevers, and Joinville convened in 1104.

King Bauduoin I captures Sidon with the help of King Sigurd of Norway, the first European King to visit the Holy Land.

Muslim-held Tripoli falls to Crusaders after a 2000-day siege. Most Muslim civilians are sold as slaves with the rest expelled and their possessions seized.

Count Hugues de Champagne marries Elizabeth de Varais, his second marriage.

Roman Catholics recognize Byzantine Christian authority in Antioch, settling years of disputes.

Louis VI, son of Philippe I, becomes King of France upon his father's death. |
|---|---|
| 1109 | Upon the death of Alberic, Etienne Harding, a close colleague of Count Hugues de Champagne, becomes Abbot at Citeaux. |
| 1110 | Crusaders destroy Beirut and its population.

Toledo blossoms as a center for the transmission of Islamic culture and science to Europe. Under the supervision of Archdeacon Domenico Gundisalvi, and with the cooperation of Johannes ben David, the translation school of the Archbishop of Toledo renders into Latin and Hebrew a large number of Arabic works on mathematics, science, and philosophy. Among the scholars are Gerard of Cremona (1117- 1187), John of Seville, Arabic specialist Adelard of Bath (1070-1146), Robert of Chester, Rudolf of Bruges and Hermann of Carinthia, Michael Scot, Stephenson of Saragossa, William of Lunis and Philip of Tripoli. |

It is possible that Toledo's translators provided researchers at Troyes with help to document the possibility of sacred artifacts and treasure under the Temple Mount in Jerusalem.

1111   Death of Abu Hamid Muhammad al-Ghazali (born 1058), one of the brightest Muslim theologians. His extensive writings include <u>The Incoherence of the Philosophers</u>, an attack on rationalism.

1112   In March, Bernard de Fontaine (1090-1153) leaves his home with 30 relatives, including his father and four brothers, Bartholomew, Andrew, Guy and Gerard, to join Abbot Etienne Harding at the near-bankrupt Cistercian monastery at Citeaux. Bernard will become the most influential spiritual leader of the Cistercians -- and later one of the most widely respected and influential men in the world. He will later be recognized as a saint – Saint Bernard.

Friar Gerard de Martigues founds the Knights of Malta.

If translation research at Troyes determined the need for a mission to Jerusalem, Bernard's creation of this special abbey could have been the European headquarters for planning, travel, and excavation operations.

Chapter Three: Beginnings

Orthodox historians place the founding of the Templars somewhere between 1114 and 1118, when the nine left for Jerusalem. This assumes such founding was a formal moment, much like the dedication of a new bridge or tunnel. Of more interest than pinpointing that exact moment, however, is decoding the chain of events leading to it.

Their publicly stated purpose was the protection of pilgrims traveling to the Holy Land. However, there is little evidence such a common task was their *real* function. Nine men just cannot protect many pilgrims along hundreds of miles of land. And simple monks, bound to vows of poverty, did not receive the kind of rich support, housing, and recognition given by Jerusalem King Bauduoin II – or later by the Pope.

If the Templars were not protecting pilgrims, what were they up to for nine years? The prevailing explanation is archeological, that they were there to dig under Solomon's Temple, to retrieve treasure and artifacts revealed by Arabic scrolls translated by monks in Toledo or France.

1113   Pope Paschal II approves the expansion of the Sovereign Order of Saint John of Jerusalem (a.k.a. Hospitallers) from a small Amalfi hospital group formed in 1070. Their first Grand Master is Peter Gérard.

According to The Knights Templar, Templars install Hugues de Payns as Grand Master on February 15, 1113 in Champagne.

According to the Principality of Seborga's official website, Bernard de Fontaine establishes a monastery in Castrum Sepulchri (now called Seborga) in northern Italy to protect a "great secret." This monastery, under the direction of Prince Abbot Edouard, includes two monks who will be future Templars, Gondemare and Rossal.

1114   Count Hugues de Champagne receives a letter from Bishop Ivo of Chartres (dies 1115) saying "We have heard that ... before leaving for Jerusalem you made a vow to join 'la Milice du Christ,' that you wish to enroll in this evangelical soldiery." La Milice du Christ (a.k.a. Soldiers of Christ) is a name by which the Knights Templar are known and the name by which Bernard de Fontaine often refers to them. This letter establishes that the Templars were organized (at least, unofficially) well before Templar historian Guillaume de Tyre's widely accepted date of 1118.

Count Hugues de Champagne and Hugues de Payns leave for their second trip to Jerusalem.

According to The Templars: Knights of God, Michael the Syrian, Patriarch of the Syriac Church at Antioch and chronicler of the Crusades, attest that Hugues de Payns was in Jerusalem for three years before founding the Templars.

1115	Count Hugues de Champagne returns from Jerusalem and provides land and funding for a new Cistercian Abbey at Clairvaux, 35 miles east of Troyes. Hugues de Payns stays behind in Jerusalem.

Death of Peter the Hermit.

Abbot of Citeaux Etienne Harding appoints Bernard de Fontaine as Abbot of Clairvaux.

The Archbishop of Cologne imprisons Tanchelm of Flanders who escapes and is later killed for preaching against the corruption of priests and encouraging people not to tithe to the Catholic Church.

King Bauduoin I builds one of the great Crusader castles, the Kerak de Montreal, in the Negev desert.

1117	In February, Bernard de Clairvaux goes to Castrum Sepulchri (Seborga) to release André de Gondemare and Rossal from their monastic vows, according Seborga's official website.

In March, King of Jerusalem Baudouin I negotiates a constitution for the Knights Templar with Hugues de Payns and Godfroi de Saint-Omer.

1118	On January 21, Pope Paschal II dies and Gelasius II takes over three days later. Holy Roman Emperor Henry V appoints his own pope, an act for which Gelasius excommunicates him.

On April 2, King Baudouin I dies of disease at El-Arish while attempting to attack Egypt.

On April 14, Baudouin du Bourg of Edessa becomes King of Jerusalem and reigns until 1131.

In September, according to Seborga's official website, Cistercian Abbot Prince Edouard of Seborga consecrates the nine original Templars in the presence of Bernard of Clairvaux and Count Hugues de Champagne. This means that de Payns must have traveled back to Seborga from Jerusalem to be with the other eight.

In November, except for Count Hugues de Champagne, all nine Templars leave for Jerusalem, arriving May 14, 1119. The principality of Seborga, located on the border of France and Italy, becomes the first and unique sovereign Cistercian state in history.

According to <u>Holy Blood, Holy Grail</u>, the Prieuré de Sion and the Templars decide to have separate Grand Masters.

Peter Gérard, Grand Master of the Hospitallers, dies and his successor Raymond de Puy increases their military role aided by Jerusalem King Baudouin II.

Templars leave Europe for Jerusalem.

1119   Pope Gelasius II dies on January 29, succeeded by Pope Callistus II (1050-1124).

On May 14, Templars arrive in Jerusalem. King Baudouin II gives the Templars the al-Aqsa mosque and the adjacent area called Solomon's Stables on the Temple Mount for a headquarters.

On Christmas Day at the Church of the Holy Sepulchre, Templars take their monastic vows from Warmund of Picquigny, the Patriarch of Jerusalem.

Pope Callistus II calls the Council of Reims which turns public opinion away from Holy Roman Emperor Henry V. Count Hugues de Champagne attends and aligns with the Pope.

Ilgazi, the Muslim Emir of Mardin (dies 1122), slaughters a large Christian army.

The Council of Toulouse condemns the Manicheans for heresy.

1120   Count Hugues de Champagne convenes a meeting in Troyes, agenda unknown.

Count Fulk V of Anjou takes an oath to join the Templars.

King Alexander I of Scotland establishes the country's first Augustinian monastery at Scone.

1121   According to The Second Messiah, Count Fulk V of Anjou travels to Jerusalem to visit the Templar excavations. He returns to Europe and grants the Templars a large endowment.

The Council of Soissons condemns Peter Abelard (1079-1142) who believes in the use of reason rather than faith to prove the Bible. Abelard's process of questioning leads the seeker to truth rather than asking him to accept it without question. "Nothing is to be believed until it is understood." -- Peter Abelard.

Death of Lambert de Saint Omer, an encyclopedist whose best-known work is a map called the Heavenly Jerusalem. He may have translated documents for Templar Geoffrey de Saint Omer from excavations under Solomon's Stables.

1122   Settling years of conflict, Pope Callistus II and Holy Roman Emperor Henry V sign the Concordat of Worms dividing power between the Pope and the Emperor.

Pope Callistus II officially recognizes the Sacred and Military Order of the Holy Sepulchre of Jerusalem.

1123   Ilgazi's nephew Balak imprisons King Baudouin II briefly.

Pope Callistus II calls the 1st Lateran Council (9th Ecumenical) in Rome which forbids simony (the selling of sacraments), forbids the marriage of priests, grants crusaders indulgences (forgiveness for their sins without punishment but usually involving payment), and discusses how to rule the Holy Land taken from the Muslims.

Count Hugues de Champagne and Elisabeth de Varais give birth to a son, Eudes I Champlitte. The Count does not believe the boy is his.

1124   King Baudouin II successfully takes Tyre from the Muslim leader Balak's forces, killing him as well. Western armies now occupy the entire coast except for Ascalon.

Honorius II becomes Pope upon the death of Callistus.

King David I brings unity of rule to Scotland and becomes King of Scots after the death of Alexander.

Death of Al-Hasan ibn al-Sabbah, leader of the Assassins.

1125   On May 14, Count Hugues de Champagne leaves his wife and son, transfers his enormous assets (4-5 times the wealth of the King of France) to his nephew Thibaud, and travels to Jerusalem to be with the Templars.

Peter DeBruys becomes extremely popular in southern France. He and his progressive followers, the Petrobrussians, believe that communion symbolizes cruelty and torture and that wine into blood is a lie; that priests may and should marry; and the fundamentalist view that religious authority comes only from literal interpretation of Scripture and not from apostolic tradition (i.e., the Pope). Catholic clergy seize and burn DeBruys at the stake in Saint Gilles in 1126.

1126　In June, Count Hugues de Champagne dies.

On October 15, King Baudouin II dies.

The Templars grow dramatically in number and create multiple enterprises. With unprecedented protection and special dispensation from the Pope, they become the world's foremost bankers, inventing the check and the branch banking system. They are the medieval world's most powerful ambassadors and statesmen, developing access, influence, and control matched only by the Pope. They are the world's prime movers in real estate, eventually controlling over 5000 properties in Scotland, Ireland, Britain, France, Spain, the German states, Hungary, and virtually every country on the Mediterranean. They finance much of the Catholic building program for 300 new places or worship including cathedrals, monasteries, and other structures.

1127　In October, Count Thibaud de Champagne (Hugues de Champagne's nephew) gives the Templars property 55 miles northwest of Troyes at Barbonne-Fayel.

Hugues de Payns donates his own properties to the Templars. Hugues' eldest brother, Edmund de Payns, inherits all the remaining family wealth.

Hugues de Payns and the Templars leave Jerusalem for Europe on the first Advent Sunday. King Baudouin II of Jerusalem gives them a letter for Bernard of Clairvaux asking his intervention with Pope Honorius II (formerly a Cistercian monk under Bernard) to sanction and fund the Templars as a military order.

According Seborga's official website, the Templars stop there on their way to France and Bernard de Clairvaux and Prince Abbot Edouard make Hugues de Payns the first Templar Grand Master. Also present is Friar Gerard de Martigues of the Knights of Malta. In that same day, the website claims, a vow of silence was made between the Knights and the Great Bishop of the Cathari to safeguard "The Great Secret."

1128   On March 19, Portuguese Queen Theresa gives the Templars the castle Soure and the town of Fonte Arcada.

In April, Hugues de Payns and the Templars travel to France to visit Count Fulk V, carrying a proposal from King Baudouin II to marry his daughter, Melissande.

Payen de Montdidier becomes Templar Grand Master for France north of the Loire river.

In late April, Hugues de Payns and Andre de Montbard travel to England where King Henry I welcomes them with large gifts of property.

Hugues de Payns sets up a Templar preceptory at London (this site is now the Holborn Underground Station). Hugh d'Argenstein is the first Grand Master for England.

Hughes de Payns and Andre de Montbard meet with King David I of Scotland (1084-1153). They also travel to Roslin, Scotland.

Hugues de Payns' wife, Catherine de Saint Clair, and her father give the Templars land at Balantrodoch for a preceptory. Hugues de Payns will have three sons: Edmund de Payns, Thibaud de Payns, and Thomas de Payns.

In September, Hugues de Payns travels to Flanders (later Belgium) to the homeland of fellow Templar Geoffroi de Saint-Omer.

King David I of Scotland builds three abbeys: Dunfermline for Benedictine monks, Holyrood Abbey in Edinburgh for Augustinian monks, and Kelso Abbey as a home for Tironensian monks relocated from an older house in Selkirk.

Cistercians establish Abbeys at Igny and Reigny in France and in England at Waverley.

In early winter, the specially convened Council of Troyes welcomes de Payns and the Templars. Those present include Templars Roland, Godefroi de Saint-Omer, Geoffroi Bisor, Payen de Montdidier, and Archambaut de Saint-Amand; Abbot Etienne Harding and Bernard de Clairvaux.

1129 On January 31 at the Council of Troyes, Pope Honorius II's legate, Matthew de Albano, gives the Templars Papal blessing of their order.

In May, Hugues de Payns returns to Jerusalem with 300 newly recruited Templars.

King Baudouin II unsuccessfully attacks Damascus with the aid of the Templars -- their first formal military mission.

Everard de Barres becomes Templar Grand Master for Barcelona, Spain.

Hugh de Rigaud becomes Templar Grand Master for southern France, based in Carcassonne.

Council of Chalons.

Count Fulk V accepts betrothal to Melissande, daughter of Jerusalem King Baudouin II and Queen Morphia of Armenia.

1130 A special conference in Toulouse gathers gifts of clothing, money, and property for the Templars.

Bernard of Clairvaux finishes In Praise of the New Knighthood about the Templars.

King Alfonso I (a.k.a. the Battler, Anfortius, Amfortas) of Aragon joins the Templars.

Council of Clermont.

On February 13, Pope Honorius II dies. Innocent II and Anacletus II (dies 1138) both claim the Papacy with Innocent II eventually fleeing to France for safety from his opponent's forces.

Troubadours and female troubadours (*trobaritz*) in the French Pyrenees pursue two themes involving the divine feminine: courtly love focused on the Goddess, the ideal woman; and adventures in search of the Holy Grail. Meanwhile, Templars and other knights influence the idea of chivalry -- the belief that a true knight is not simply a warrior for his master, but has a higher duty to protect the powerless and those less fortunate.

1131 In June, King Baudouin II dies. On September 14, Templar Count Fulk V of Anjou and Melissande become King and Queen of Jerusalem.

Council of Reims.

1132 Council of Piacenza.

1134 King Alfonso I of Aragon dies and wills an astonishing gift to the Templars - a third of his lands.

Abbot Etienne Harding dies at Citeaux on March 28. He is buried in the tomb of predecessor Alberic in the cloister.

Construction begins on the North tower of a large Cathedral at Chartres.

1135　Bernard de Clairvaux writes <u>Liber ad Milites Templi De Laude Novae Militae</u> in support of the Templars, attracting many new recruits.

Pope Innocent II calls the Council of Pisa to excommunicate anti-Pope Anacletus II and extend special favor and funding to the Templars.

1136　On May 24, Hugues de Payns dies and Robert de Craon of Burgundy (dies January 13, 1149) becomes the second Templar Grand Master.

Geoffrey of Monmouth writes the <u>History of the Kings of Britain</u>, popularizing Arthurian legends.

Rise of Henry of Lausanne (dies 1145) whose Henricians condemn Catholic clergy for their love of wealth and power. Henricians teach that the sacraments are valid only from priests dedicated to the purity of poverty. His movement spreads throughout the south of France.

1137　The Templars build their Paris preceptory on land granted by King Louis VI.

The Templars receive the Essex manor of Cressing from Matilda, Queen of England and niece of King Baudouin I of Jerusalem.

King David I builds Melrose Abbey, the first Cistercian Abbey in Scotland.

Muslims under Imad ud Din Zengi (dies 1146) capture Jerusalem King Fulk then let him go.

The Assassins take the fortress of Khariba from the Templars.

1138　Anti-Pope Anacletus II dies and is briefly replaced by new Anti-Pope Victor. Pope Innocent II returns to Rome.

King David I of Scotland builds Jedburgh Abbey in Scotland for Augustinian monks.

1139   The 2nd Lateran Council (10th Ecumenical) at Rome under Pope Innocent II and Holy Roman Emperor Conrad III condemns the Petrobrussians, the Henricians, and exiles Arnold of Brescia (dies 1155). Bernard de Clairvaux preaches against the use of lay ministers in church services. The Council enacts a stronger celibacy policy for priests, partially to prevent priests' children from inheriting Catholic property.

Thibaud de Payns, son of Hugues de Payns, becomes Abbot of Saint Columba-de-Saens.

Pope Innocent II grants a charter to the Prieuré de Sion.

Templars build castles at Port Bonnet, Baghras, and Darbask in the Holy Land.

In March, Pope Innocent II writes *Omne datum optimum*, granting the Templars exemption from the authority of local bishops, exemption from taxation by any king, release from all obedience except to the Papacy, and other quite extraordinary privileges. This is their official sanction to become the world's most powerful group.

Chapter Four:
Warriors, Monks, Bankers, Statesmen

Now fully in power, protected by the Pope, honored by nearly every landowner in Europe, and controlling what will become the world's first central bank, the Templars are in their prime. They are the most powerful political group in the world. It is truly their heyday. Kings, generals, even Popes defer to them as catalysts in an ever-expanding European economy.

Their military and economic strength grows to protect extensive holdings all over Europe and the Middle East. Templar regiments attach to Catholic armies (under various national flags) in further Papal crusades against, well, just about everyone. The next few hundred years are not a good time to be non-Christian, an intellectual, a woman -- or anyone else who threatens the male Catholic power structure. Between three and six million die in various Catholic purges, inquisitions, tortures, mobs, and other atrocities between 1209 and 1750, all in the name of Jesus.

A famous story chronicles the escalation of this senseless violence. As Catholic forces go into the city of Beziers in 1209, they ask their commander, a priest turned general named Arnaud Amaury, "How do we know whom to kill? There are so many women and children." To which, the commander replied, "Kill them all. God will know his own." The gentleness and forgiveness of Jesus has been completely twisted around into a rationale for genocide.

1140   Templars build Castel Safed in Israel.

Damascus and Jerusalem collaborate to attack the Muslim ruler of Aleppo, Zengi.

Construction begins on the Cathedral of Kilwinning in Scotland.

King David I of Scotland founds a Cistercian monastery in Newbattle.

1141   Death of Hugh of Saint Victor, Saxon philosopher and theologian, who defined faith as "about things absent, above opinion and below science."

Bernard de Clairvaux at the Council of Sens condemns the writing of Peter Abelard. The vocal support of one of Abelard's more radical students, the infamous Arnold of Brescia, does not help his credibility with Catholic leaders.

1142   Many Bogomils burn at the stake for heresy in Cologne, Germany.

French King Louis VII starts a war by seizing the properties of Count Thybald of Champagne. Bernard de Clairvaux intercedes and settles the dispute.

King David I of Scotland founds a Cistercian abbey in Dundrennan.

1143	Pope Innocent II dies, replaced by Celestine II, who issues *Milites Templi*, essentially the same sweeping support of the Templars as *Omne datum optimum.*
	Beginning construction of the Cathedral of Notre Dame in Paris.
	Templars build Castle Karak (in modern-day Jordan) as a prison and to control the roads between Damascus and Egypt.
	Upon the death of his father, Fulk, Baudouin III (1130-1163) becomes King of Jerusalem at age 13, crowned with his mother, Queen Melissande, as regent. He will later marry Theodora Comnena, niece of the Byzantine Emperor.
	Peter the Venerable at Cluny translates the *Qur'an* into Latin.
1144	Pope Celestine II dies, replaced by Lucius II, who issues his version of *Milites Templi*, again reaffirming the *Omne datum optimum.*
	On December 24, Muslims under Zengi captures many Templar castles plus Edessa, where there is an especially brutal killing of 5,000 Catholics. Their deaths create a call for a Second Crusade.
1145	Pope Lucius II dies and is replaced by Eugenius III (dies 1153), a Cistercian monk and colleague of Bernard de Clairvaux. Eugenius III issues a fourth version of *Omne datum optimum* called *Militia Dei.*
	Bernard de Clairvaux arrives in southern France to convert the Cathari to Catholicism. While disliking Catharism as a doctrine and expecting to find vile heretics, he instead finds the Cathari to be loving, gentle, peace-loving people. He worries, however, about the pervasive acceptance of Cathari practices such as allowing women as clergy, or *parfaites*.

1146   On March 1, Pope Eugenius III calls for a second crusade. It is launched on Easter Sunday by Bernard de Clairvaux, Pope Eugenius III, and King Louis VII of France at Vézélay. It is agreed that the crusade will leave one year later. Queen Eleanor of Aquitane (1122-1204), wife of Louis VII, is so moved by Bernard's speech that she vows to go on the crusade herself, a novel idea for a woman at the time.

Other crusaders include:

1. Robert, Count of Dreux, brother of King Louis VII
2. Alfonso-Jordan, Count of Toulouse
3. William, Count of Nevers
4. Thierry, Count of Flanders, married to the stepdaughter of Jerusalem Queen Melissande
5. Henry of Flanders
6. Amadeus, Count of Savoy
7. Archimbald, Count of Bourbon

Arnold of Brescia comes to power in Rome and drives Pope Eugenius III out of town for eight years, a remarkable feat for a grassroots movement. Arnold believes Catholics should conform fully to the original ideals of Jesus and criticizes Catholic Bishops for their wealth and dishonesty. He insists that clergy acknowledge spirit is not worldly and renounce all material power -- land and money -- a noble but very unpopular request.

Zengi is murdered and succeeded by his son, Nur al-Din.

1147 Templars under Master of France Everard des Barres accompany the sizable forces of German King Conrad III and King Louis VII on the Second Crusade, which leaves from France and with difficulty makes it to Jerusalem via Antioch, where Eleanor's uncle Prince Raymond de Poitiers welcomes them. Along with Eleanor of Aquitaine are her courtiers Sybelle, Mamille, Florine, and Faydide. Although Eleanor wants to stay in Antioch, Louis VII takes her by force to Jerusalem.

Catholic forces in Portugal expel the Muslims.

1148 Malachi O'More of Ireland (born 1094), known for his prophecies about future Popes, dies in the arms of Bernard at Clairvaux. Malachi predicts there will only be 112 more Popes (Pope John Paul II is 110 or 111, depending on how you count).

On June 24, Jerusalem King Baudouin III, Holy Roman Emperor Conrad III, French King Louis VII, Hospitallers, Templars, and other crusaders decide to attack Damascus in Syria, their only real Muslim ally. By July 28, after repeated humiliating defeats, Catholic forces withdraw.

Council of Reims.

Hildegard of Bingen (1098-1179), one of the few women mystics approved by the Catholic Church, corresponds at length with Bernard of Clairvaux on her beautiful visions, writings, and illustrations. She founds a monastery at Rupertsburg.

Catholics capture Tortosa in Spain from the Muslims.

1149   King Louis VII returns to Europe from the Second Crusade defeated. Blaming failure to overcome the Muslims on the Eastern Orthodox Christians at Constantinople, he calls for another crusade - against them. He also loses the affection of wife Eleanor of Aquitane which means a potential loss of an enormous dowry of money and property in France.

Templars take control of Gaza.

Everard de Barres becomes Grand Master of the Templars upon the death of Robert de Craon.

1150   At the Council of Chartres, Bernard de Clairvaux calls for a third crusade but after the defeat of the second there is no interest.

1152   Henri I becomes the Count of Champagne until his death in 1181.

Upon the resignation of Everard de Barres to join the Cistercian monastery at Clairvaux, Bernard de Trémélai becomes Grand Master of the Templars.

In May, just months after her marriage to King Louis VII of France is annulled, Eleanor of Aquitaine marries Henry d'Anjou who becomes King Henry II of England in 1154.

King Baudouin III of Jerusalem tires of his mother's regency and they quarrel constantly. To resolve their differences, they decide to divide the kingdom.

By now Cistercians have built an amazing 350 abbeys, up from 7 in 1118.

1153 In July, upon the death of Bernard de Trémélai in battle against the Muslim fortress at Ascalon, original Templar André de Montbard becomes the 5th Grand Master.

On August 20, Bernard de Clairvaux dies.

Construction begins on the Notre Dame cathedral in Paris.

Muslim Nur al-Din takes control of Damascus.

Pope Eugenius III dies and Anastasius IV takes office for a year, during which he officially recognizes the Order of Malta.

1154 King Baudouin III and his mother Queen Melissande resolve their differences. She retires to a convent in Bethany run by her sister the Abbess Joveta.

1155 Pope Hadrian IV (1105~1159, the only English Pope) and Emperor Frederick I Barbarossa retake Rome from Arnold of Brescia and hang him as a warning to other heretics. Later, Hadrian and Frederick I will quarrel over Papal supremacy.

1156　On January 17, upon the decision of Andre de Montbard to become a monk at Clairvaux, Bertrand de Blanquefort becomes the 6th Grand Master and gives the Templars title to many of his lands at Rennes-le-Château in France.

According to <u>Holy Blood, Holy Grail,</u> Templars under Grand Master de Blanquefort import German miners for a massive digging operation at Pech Cardou near Serres, the site of an old Roman gold mine. To maintain secrecy, the miners are forbidden to interact with the local community. Cesar d'Arcons, an engineer surveying the site in the 17th century, concludes the German miners were not *mining* -- they were putting something in.

Henry St. Clair is appointed as Ambassador to England by King David I.

Founding of the Order of Alcantera, Spanish warrior/monks based on the Knights Templars with a mission of reconquering the Iberian peninsula away from the Muslims.

According to <u>The Templars</u>, Prince of Antioch Reynald de Chatillon attacks Byzantine-held Cyprus in anger at Byzantine Emperor Manuel Comnenus. Not caring that the island's inhabitants were Christian, "their women were raped, their children and old people murdered, their churches and convents robbed, their cattle and crops sequestered."

1157　Muslims imprison Templar Grand Master Bertrand de Blanquefort after his unsuccessful attack on Muslim territory.

1158   King Baldwin III marries Theodora, Byzantine Emperor Manuel's niece. Her large dowry replenishes the kingdom's treasury.

Founding of the Order of Calatrava, Spanish warrior/monks based on the Templars with a mission of reconquering the Iberian peninsula from the Muslims.

1159   Pope Alexander III (1100-1181) takes office and declares exclusive right to confer sainthood, taking this privilege away from local bishoprics.

Marie, daughter of Eleanor of Aquitane and King Louis VII of France, marries Count Henry I of Champagne.

Through a treaty and ransom negotiated by Byzantine Emperor Manuel Comnenus, the Muslims release Templar Grand Master Bertrand de Blanquefort.

1160   Portuguese Templar Master Gualdim Pais (dies 1195) builds the *Convento de Christ* (Castle Ceras) in Tomar, Portugal with a large eight-sided chapel.

Muslims under the Governor of Aleppo ambush Prince of Antioch Reynald de Chatillon and imprison him for 16 years. No Christians come forward to provide his ransom.

1161   The London Templar preceptory moves to a new location between Fleet Street and the Thames River.

1162   Pope Alexander III issues another <u>Omne Datum Optimum</u> in support of the Templars.

1163   Amalric I (a.k.a. Amaury, Baudouin III's brother) becomes King of Jerusalem until 1174.

The Council of Tours denounces the Cathari.

Shirkuh, Nur al-Din's top officer, takes control of Egypt briefly and passes control to his nephew, Saladin (a.k.a. Salah-al-Din Yusuf ibn-Ayyub, 1138-1193).

1164   On January 30, King Henry II calls a Council of Clarendon in England to determine laws regarding Church and state. Some of his decisions cause a rift with Archbishop of Canterbury Thomas Becket. Richard de Hastings, English Templar Grand Master, attempts to reconcile their differences.

1165   Alarmed by the Cathari's growing influence, the Council of Albi in France condemns them as does the Council of Lombez.

Eleanor leaves King Henry II and returns to her homeland in Aquitane.

1166   In the dead of winter, authorities in England capture, torture, and send out in the cold some thirty Cathari missionaries.

1167   The Cathari Grand Council at Saint Felix de Lauragais (near Toulouse), under the influence of the Bogomil leader Nicetas from Constantinople, formally adopts the belief in dualism between good and evil. The Council sets up bishoprics for the surrounding area and steps up competition with the Catholic Church.

1168   On January 2, Bertrand de Blanquefort dies and Philip de Milly of Nablus becomes the 7th Grand Master of the Templars. He refuses King of Jerusalem's Amalric's request for the Templars to attack Egypt again.

Amalric turns instead to the Hospitallers and they attack the city of Belbeis, slaughtering the entire population. This atrocity energizes the young Sultan Saladin who will later drive the West from all of Palestine. Historian Charles Addison notes that because of "the unjustifiable expedition of King Amalric and the Hospitallers against the infidels, the powerful talents of the young Kurdish chieftain would in all probability never [have] developed."

1170 Saladin invades the border areas of Palestine with 40,000 troops. The Muslim victory motivates the Pope to issue *Omni Datum Optimum* giving the Templars extraordinary privileges, including exemption from taxation and the right to give the excommunicated religious services once a year.

Eleanor of Aquitaine and her daughter Countess Marie of Champagne (by French King Louis VII) set up a school to teach poetry and courtly love in Poitiers. About the same time, Lambert le Begue creates an order of laywomen, the Beguines, who commit to the monastic life but without traditional monastic vows -- or the requirement of a dowry (as in convents). The Beguines are Quietists who believe that union with God comes from quiet, spiritual, contemplation; sex (if chosen) is a form of union with God; and use local-language scriptures rather than depending on the priesthood for translation.

Four knights decide that upon hearing King Henry II's anger with Thomas Becket, they will kill Becket on December 29. The knights are sentenced to 14 years with the Templars in the Holy Land. King Henry donates money for their support.

Founding of the Order of Caceres, which changes into the Order of Santiago (a.k.a. Military Order of Saint James of the Sword) by 1175. These are Spanish warrior/monks at Santiago de Compostela, a shrine to James the brother of Jesus.

1171　de Milly resigns and Odo de Saint-Amand becomes the 8th Templar Grand Master.

Abu l-Walid Muhammad ibn Ahmad Ibn Rushd (a.k.a. Averroes, 1126-1198), Muslim philosopher and advisor to a series of Caliphs, becomes Kadi of Cordoba. Averroes is an expert on Aristotle as well as medicine, astronomy, and religion. In 1180, he will write <u>The Incoherence of the Incoherence</u> about the fusion of Neo-Platonism, Aristotelian philosophy, and Islam. Although he consistently advanced the idea of one truth (as contained in the <u>Qur'an</u>), Averroes believed, unlike his Muslim brethren, in the equality of men and women as equal participation increases an economy.

Saladin overthrows the Fatimids and increases his territory in Egypt.

1173　The Waldensian (a.k.a. the Vaudois) movement at Lyons defies Pope Alexander III by having lay people (including women) teach and read the <u>Bible</u> and perform sacraments (only Catholic priests have these privileges). Leader Peter Valdes bases his movement on scriptural authority and not that of the Papacy. The Waldensians believe that anything that serves to separate them from material wealth brings them closer to God. Valdes renounces wealth believing that suffering from being poor is good for the soul. He and his followers believe true virtue is demonstrating love and care for mankind. Valdes goes to Rome to obtain papal approval for his order, but Pope Alexander III condemns him.

The sons of King Henry II of England rebel and confine Eleanor of Aquitane on charges of conspiring with the French.

1174   Pope Alexander III recognizes Bernard de Clairvaux as a Saint.

King Amalric dies of typhus and dysentery. His son by his first wife (and cousin) Agnes of Courtenay, Baudouin IV, becomes King of Jerusalem at age 13 with Count Raimond III of Tripoli as regent.

Muslim leader Nur ed-Din dies with Saladin taking over his Kingdom.

1175   Publication of <u>Sefer ha-Bahir (Book of Brilliance)</u> in Provence. This classic work on Kabbalistic philosophy (Jewish esoteric mysticism) first mentions the idea of a "tree of life" and sets the stage for the growth of Jewish mysticism in Septimania (see Map 6). Kabbalists circumvent the Jewish doctrine of only one God by a complex assortment of names for various elements of God – and by believing the creator and the created are one. This is a major problem for traditional Jews and Catholics who fear such beliefs place too much emphasis on the self. Kabbalists claim a "secret knowledge" of God through sacred texts containing special arrangements and anagrams of Hebrew letters, claiming these have special power when spoken or written.

On July 3, Pope Alexander III approves the Order of Santiago in <u>Benedictus Deus</u>. By 1186 the Order of Santiago has lands in Toledo, Palmella, and later in Italy, England, France, and Palestine.

1176   Seljuk Turks under Sultan Kilij Arslän II successfully attack the Byzantine stronghold of Anatolia.

The Governor of Aleppo releases former Prince of Antioch Reynaud del Chatillon in exchange for King Baldwin IV's help to attack Saladin.

Monk and former Templar Grand Master Everard de Barres dies at Clairvaux.

1177 On November 1, Templars under Saint-Amand nearly kill Saladin in his tent but he escapes.

Pope Alexander III confirms the Order of Alcantera.

Coptic Christians from Ethiopia arrive in Jerusalem to request an altar in the Holy City. Their request goes answered by the Pope.

1178 Pope Alexander III officially confirms and condones the Prieuré de Sion's possessions.

1179 In April, the Templars complete building a castle at Jacob's Ford (a.k.a. Chastelet). By August, Saladin completely destroys it and captures Templar Grand Master Odo de Saint-Amand. Refusing ransom, Saint-Amand dies in prison in Damascus.

At the 3rd Lateran Council (11th Ecumenical) Pope Alexander III and Holy Roman Emperor Frederick I Barbarossa condemn the Cathari and Waldensians and launch an educational campaign to discredit both groups. With encouragement from Templar critic Guillaume de Tyre, the Council admonishes the Templars and the Hospitallers to stick strictly to monastic vows. They also decree that Jews wear identifying badges, observe strict curfews, live only in certain areas, and be forbidden from government and trade positions.

About this time, Chrétien de Troyes (1144-1190) writes the first Holy Grail epics under sponsorship of Countess Marie de Champagne at Troyes.

1180	Count Henri de Champagne, Marie's husband, travels to Jerusalem to fight the Muslims.
	Death of Abraham Ibn Daud (born 1110), Spanish Jewish philosopher and historian, in Toledo. He attempts a synthesis of Judaism and Aristotelianism and writes the book <u>Sefer ha-Kabbalah (Book of Tradition)</u>.
	Sometime in the 1180's, Guillaume de Tyre writes the first outsider history of the Templars.
	King of Jerusalem Baudouin IV's sister, Sibylla, marries future successor Guy de Lusignan. King Baudouin IV and Saladin agree to a two-year peace treaty.
	On October 8, Arnold de Toroga, Templar Master in Spain, becomes the 9th Grand Master of the Templars. He leaves for Europe with Hospitaller Grand Master Roger des Moulins and Jerusalem Patriarch Heraclius to seek financial and military help from Italy, England, and France to fight Saladin.
1181	Reynald de Chatillon breaks the peace by attacking a Muslim caravan, causing Saladin to imprison 1500 Catholic pilgrims shipwrecked off the Egyptian coast.
	Henri II succeeds Thibaud as Count de Champagne.
	Heraclius consecrates the Templar preceptory in London.
1182	Reynald de Chatillon takes on Saladin through a brilliant and bold new strategy - building ships, hauling them over land to the Red Sea, and attacking Muslim pilgrims to Mecca. Saladin's brother Malik thwarts de Chatillon just as he was planning to steal Muhammad's body from Mecca.
	King Philippe II exiles the Jews from France.
1183	Reynald de Chatillon escapes from Saladin who publicly vows to find him and kill him.

1184	Pope Lucius III (1110-1185) issues an Inquisition against the Cathari which has little impact. He also excommunicates the Waldensians and the Humiliati, Italians who believe in a life of simple work and prayer.

The Council of Verona condemns the Cathari and the remaining Arnoldists.

Saladin and the Assassins form an alliance against the Templars and other Christian military orders.

In a rare defection, English Templar Robert of St. Albans fights for Saladin, leading Muslim forces against Christian-held Jerusalem.

On September 30, Templar Grand Master Arnold de Toroga dies in Verona. |
| 1185 | On March 16, King Baudouin IV dies, weakened by leprosy, without a wife or direct heir. King Baudouin IV's seven-year-old nephew by his sister Sibylla, Baudouin V, becomes King of Jerusalem. Raimond III of Tripoli, former regent for Bauduoin IV, becomes recent for Bauduoin V and negotiates a four-year peace treaty with Saladin.

According to Graham Hancock, Templars accompany the exiled Prince Lalibela from Jerusalem to Axum in Ethiopia where legend says the Ark of the Covenant resides in the Church of St Mary of Zion where only deacons are allowed to enter.

Saladin takes back Castle Karak from the Templars.

Gerard de Ridefort becomes the 10th Templar Grand Master. |
| 1186 | In August, King Baudouin V dies and Queen Sibylla's second husband, Guy de Lusignan becomes King of Jerusalem. Meanwhile, Reynald de Chatillon engages Saladin by continuing to kill and plunder Muslim caravans. |

1187　In May, Saladin's son crosses the Jordan river and successfully defeats Templar and Hospitaller forces, beheading all of them.

On July 4, Saladin and an 80,000-strong Muslim army defeat the Catholics under Reynald de Chatillon, Gerard de Ridefort, and King Guy de Lusignan at Hattin near Jerusalem. Saladin personally beheads Reynald de Chatillon for his previous attacks on Muslim caravans. The "True Cross" passes to the Muslims, who according to legend take it to Damascus. There, Muslim tradition has it moving to Baghdad to be symbolically trampled by Muslim feet.

Saladin spares Gerard de Ridefort, but orders the execution of 230 other Templars. On July 10, he takes Acre without a fight. On September 4, Ascalon surrenders. Saladin goes on to defeat Jaffa, Sidon, and Beirut. King Guy de Lusignan is released. Gerard de Ridefort is imprisoned and later released.

Saladin begins a siege of Jerusalem on September 20.

On October 2, Saladin conquers Jerusalem and takes the al-Aqsa mosque from the Templars. Rather than killing everyone, he ransoms 20,000 Catholics inside the city. He reclaims the Temple of Solomon for Muslims. Most other Catholic strongholds fall to Saladin, except for Antioch, Tripoli, and Tyre.

Pope Urban III dies suddenly at Ferrara on receiving the news that Saladin took Jerusalem. Clement III becomes Pope, returns to Rome, and make amends with Holy Roman Emperor Frederick I Barbarossa.

The Order of Alcantera merges with the Order of Santiago.

1188 Defeated Templars regroup in Antioch.

According to Baigent, Lincoln, and Leigh in <u>Holy Blood, Holy Grail</u>, during a meeting between King Henry II of England and King Philippe II of France to discuss the situation in Jerusalem, the "cutting of the elm" incident splits the Templars and the Prieuré de Sion into separate organizations with separate Grand Masters. This event happens at the Templar preceptory at Gisors, France. Jean de Gisors (1133-1220) is named first Grand Master of the Prieuré de Sion.

1189 On May 11, Holy Roman Emperor Frederick I Barbarossa leaves for the 3rd Crusade, drowning on the trip to Jerusalem.

In July, at the coronation of King Richard I (1157-1199) of England, a mob angry at the wealth of the Jews massacres many of them.

Saladin grants Coptic Christians from Ethiopia a site for their altar in Jerusalem.

On October 4, King Guy de Lusignan has Gerard de Ridefort lay siege to Acre. Saladin again captures de Ridefort -- and this time kills him.

Eleanor of Aquitaine regains her freedom from confinement upon the death of King Henry II and serves as regent for her son Richard I, who grants the Templars a charter of special privileges.

1190 On July 4, new allies King Richard I and French King Philippe II start their version of the 3rd Crusade against Muslim-held Jerusalem.

Creation in Jerusalem of the Teutonic Knights of Saint Mary's Hospital.

1191   On May 12, King Richard I marries Princess Berengaria of Navarre aboard a ship outside of Cyprus. On the 13th, he and King Guy de Lusignan of Palestine successfully attack Cyprus and rescue hostages taken by renegade Byzantine Prince Isaac Ducas Comnenus, an ally of Saladin.

Robert de Sablé becomes the 11th Grand Master of the Templars and buys Cyprus from King Richard I for 100,000 besants.

On July 12, King Richard I defeats the Muslims at Acre and negotiates a ransom for its citizens of 200,000 besants, the return of Catholic prisoners, and the return of the "True Cross."

On August 20, King Richard I, in an incredible act of brutality, executes 2700 Muslim citizens in Acre.

1192   Henry I of Champagne is voted King of Jerusalem, although he is never crowned.

The Templars return Cyprus to King Richard I who sells it to Jerusalem King Guy de Lusignan.

On September 2, tired of their many battles, King Richard I, Henry I of Champagne, Robert de Sablé, and Saladin sign a five-year peace treaty and their armies disband.

1193   On the journey back to Europe, King Richard I is captured Duke of Austria Leopold V and later imprisoned by Holy Roman Emperor Henry VI.

Robert de Sablé dies and on September 28, Gilbert Erail (a.k.a. Gilbert Horal) becomes the 12th Templar Grand Master.

In the spring, Saladin dies in Damascus and the Muslim empire divides between his brother al-Adil and other heirs.

1194 King Richard I is released in February.

1195 King Richard I arranges for the marriage of his sister Joanna to Count Raimond IV de Toulouse.

1197 Thibaud III becomes Count de Champagne until 1201.

1198 German Catholics form the Teutonic Knights as a monastic order in the Holy Land. They adopt the Templar rule, but wear a black cross on their white habits instead of a red cross.

Countess Marie de Champagne dies.

1199 Pope Innocent III (1161-1216) supports the Templars by reaffirming *Omne Datum Optimum* eight times. He creates a vision of reuniting the Catholic and Eastern Orthodox churches and increases the power of the Papacy, declaring in *Vergentis* that heretics must be executed like any other traitors.

King Richard I dies on April 6.

1200 Pope Innocent III reinstates the Humiliati after they recant.

1201 Thibaud IV becomes Count de Champagne for a record 52 years until 1253. He has only one child, Jeanne (1274-1305) who will marry the future French King Philippe IV le Bel.

Philip de Plessiez becomes the 13th Grand Master of the Templars.

1202 Pope Innocent III launches the 4th Crusade against the Egyptians and the Bogomils in Bosnia. Some Bogomils flee to Europe, particularly to sympathetic Cathari communities in southern France.

1203 Fortification of Montségur, a mountaintop Cathari fortress for women in southern France, in anticipation of a Catholic attack.

In August, French crusader Robert de Clari (1170-1216) reports on a shroud with the image of Jesus at Our Lady Holy Mary Church of Blachernae, near Constantinople.

1204 In February, Catholics and Cathars debate in Carcassonne under the sponsorship of King Peter II of Aragon.

On April 6, Venice attacks the Eastern Orthodox capital of Constantinople which allows their peaceful entry after promising ransom. Templars go on the trip but refuse to fight against other Christians.

On April 13, after Constantinople fails to produce the money, Catholic forces spend three days conducting particularly gruesome orgies, riots, and mass killings that eliminate any chance of east-west reconciliation. Robert de Clari and others loot sacred sites and take at least 54 relics back to Rome.

According to Ian Wilson in The Jesus Conspiracy, Eastern Emperor Baldwin I sends the Shroud of Turin along with substantial treasure to Rome as a gift to the Pope under the care of a Templar envoy named Baroche. Six Genoese ships, known for their cruelty, attack the envoy's vessel, take the treasure, but uncharacteristically leave ship and crew unharmed. Wilson believes this was a setup to pass the Shroud into the hands of the Templars.

On May 16, Count Baldwin IX of Flanders is crowned as Baldwin I, Eastern Emperor.

1206 Cathari Council at Mirepoix.

Cistercian monk Dominic Guzman (1170-1221) establishes a Catholic asylum to convert Cathari women (obviously they must be crazy to reject Catholicism!).

1207 Two-week religious debate in Montreal between Cathari, represented by Arnaud Hot and Guilhabert de Castres, and Catholics, represented by Dominic Guzman and papal representative Pierre de Castelnau.

Meeting in Palmiers between Catholics and Waldensians. According to legend, Esclarmonde de Foix attends as hostess. She is told by the Catholics to be quiet and not take part in a debate meant for men. Later, she becomes a *parfait* and military leader in the Cathari movement.

On May 29, Pope Innocent III excommunicates Count Raimond VI de Toulouse for showing too much tolerance to the Cathari.

1208 On January 15, henchmen of the Count Raimond VI de Toulouse murder Papal legate Pierre de Castelnau in Saint-Gilles. Pope Innocent III attributes the crime to the Count's association with the Cathari.

Pope Innocent III admonishes the Templars for their behavior, specifically mentioning necromancy (summoning and communicating with the dead).

1209   On February 12, Templar Grand Master Philip de Plessiez dies in a battle with the Muslims. Guillaume de Chartres becomes the 14th Grand Master of the Templars.

On June 18, Cathari sympathizer Count Raimond VI de Toulouse is publicly whipped at Saint-Gilles and reverts to Catholicism.

On June 24 (John the Baptist's feast day), the Albigensian Crusade against the Cathari begins in Lyons with 6,000 and 30,000 troops under command of the Abbot of Citeaux, Arnaud Amaury (a.k.a. Arnoldus, 1160-1225). The June crusade begins what Richard Leigh called the "first case of genocide in European history."

On July 22 (Mary Magdalene's feast day) in Beziers, Catholic forces kill over 200 Cathari plus 15,000 to 20,000 Catholics who insist on protecting them. The genocide continues as they defeat Perpignan, Narbonne, Carcassonne, and Toulouse, killing most everyone in sight, Catholics and Cathari alike. However, they are unable to take the Cathari at the fortress of Montségur.

On August 15, Catholic forces take Carcassonne. Albi, Castres, Caussade, Fanjeaux, and other French towns soon follow.

In September, the Council of Avignon denounces heretics and Jews.

Francis of Assisi (1181-1226) starts the Franciscan order of monks at Vézelay, France. Francis leads lay people in voluntary poverty through traveling and preaching. Although he criticizes Catholic failure to live up to the ideals of Scripture, he receives Papal approval for his considerable humility and not rejecting the Pope's authority.

1210   On July 22, Catholic forces under Simon de Montfort (dies 1264) defeat the Cathari. At Minerve in August, 140 people leap into the flames rather than convert.

In September, Papal legates excommunicate Count Raimond VI de Toulouse a second time.

On November 23, Catholic Simon de Montfort defeats Termes after a nine-month siege. He destroys the Chateau de Blanchefort near Serres.

1211   On May 3, Catholic forces defeat Lavaur and burn over 400 Cathari. They throw *parfaite* Giraude de Lavaur into a well and stone her to death. She owned large tracts of land, a privilege unheard of in the rest of Europe, and one thought evil by the Papacy.

1212   Clare of Assisi (born 1194) starts the Order of Poor Clares.

In the tragic "Children's Crusade," over 50,000 children go on crusade to the Holy Land where their pureness of heart is to recapture it for the Catholics. Unfortunately, most of them drown or are sold into slavery by corrupt merchants. This crusade is the origin of the "Pied Piper" story.

1213   The Council of St. Albans creates what will become the English Parliament.

1215   Dominic Guzman begins the Dominican order of monks at Toulouse. Dressed in black, they overcome heresy through preaching and conversion rather than force. They eventually yield to becoming Papal police, using their influence and authority to give divine permission to the tortures of the Inquisition.

Signing of the Magna Carta by King John in England. Also present is Aymeric St. Mawr, English Templar Grand Master.

On November 11, Pope Innocent III convenes in Rome the 4th Lateran Council (12th Ecumenical), saying "there is but one Universal Church of the faithful, outside of which no one at all is saved." He approves the Dominican order of monks, condemns the Cathari, and decrees all re-baptizers be punished by death. He formalizes transubstantiation and requires Muslims and Jews to wear specially marked clothing to keep Catholics from being "fooled" into marrying them. Finally, he prohibits trial by ordeal (but specifically does not prohibit torture during interrogation), saying "Use against heretics the spiritual sword of excommunication, and if this does not prove effective, use the material sword."

1217 Launch of the dismal 5th Crusade from Cyprus (then the main home of the Templars) against the Egyptians.

Construction starts on Castle Pilgrim at Atlit.

1218 On June 25, according to legend, Catholic commander and misogynist Simon de Montfort is killed during the Toulouse siege by a heavy weapon -- operated by a woman.

The Templars begin building the Castle Pilgrim, the strongest of all their fortresses in the Holy Land, at Atlit.

Pope Honorius III (dies 1227) directs a crusade against the Muslims in Spain.

The Knights Templar Chronology

1219   Catholic forces take Toulouse and much of the Languedoc area of France searching for Cathari and other heretics.

Francis of Assisi negotiates a startling deal with the Sultan al-Kamil of Cairo. In exchange for leaving Egypt, the Sultan promises to give the Catholics Jerusalem, Galilee, all of central Palestine, and to top it off, the True Cross. Amazingly, the Catholics decline believing they should not negotiate with Muslims no matter how good the terms.

On August 25, Guillaume de Chartres dies and Pedro de Montaigu, former Grand Master in Spain and Provence, becomes the 15th Templar Grand Master.

1220   Friedrich II is crowned Holy Roman Emperor. Compared with previous leaders he is a maverick, preferring to resolve disputes by negotiation rather than by force. His admiration for Islam and his near-contempt for hypocritical Catholic behavior make him one of the most innovative, successful, and scorned rulers in Europe. Friedrich is also an accomplished scholar, with a formidable library and a dazzling collection of translators, scholars, poets, and astrologers. Trained in Arabic and Muslim customs, he is an excellent diplomat for nearly anywhere in the world.

According to _Holy Blood, Holy Grail,_ Marie de Saint-Clair becomes Grand Master of the Prieuré de Sion.

1221   On July 12, still determined to conquer Egypt, the Catholics lose to Sultan al-Kamil, who offers a sweet deal: leave Egypt, and accept an eight-year truce, and get back the "True Cross" upon which Jesus was crucified. After a resounding military defeat, Catholics accept the deal and leave. However, the Sultan does not deliver the "True Cross."

1222   The Council of Oxford.

1223 Templars feud with Henry III of England over their refusal to pay taxes and their influence with judges. The Pope issues *De Insolentia Templariorium Reprimenda* but the rebuke has no effect. Henry III later warms up to the Templars and calls on them for help in various diplomatic missions.

1224 Holy Roman Emperor Friedrich II starts the University of Naples, one of the first in Europe.

1225 The Council of Bourges

1226 King Louis VIII dies and his 12-year-old son Louis IX is crowned, with mother Queen Blanche of Castille (1188-1252) as regent.

A Cathar Council meets at Pieusse.

1227 Pope Gregory IX (1155~1241) excommunicates Friedrich II for covertly plotting against the Papacy.

1228 On June 26, the now-excommunicated Holy Roman Emperor Friedrich II (1194-1250) launches a 6th Crusade against Egyptian forces in Jerusalem. He lands in Acre on September 7. Because of his status with Pope Gregory IX, Templars and Hospitallers mistrust him and the alliance is uneasy.

1229 On February 18, Holy Roman Emperor Friedrich II negotiates a 10-year peace treaty with the Egyptian Sultan al-Kamil and is crowned King of Jerusalem March 18. However, despite these results, Pope Gregory IX excommunicates Friedrich II again for "collaboration" with the Muslims and attacks his properties in Italy.

On April 12, Count Raimond VII de Toulouse (dies 1249) affects a temporary cease-fire between the Cathari and the Catholics through negotiations (the Treaty of Miaux) with his cousin Queen Blanche of Castille. Soon, under pressure, he will reluctantly turn against the Cathari.

On May 1, Holy Roman Emperor Friedrich II is forced to leave the Holy Land to defend Papal attacks on his lands in Italy.

In November, the Council of Toulouse meets to decide the spiritual fate of the Cathari, setting up a system of Catholic-supervised, local tribunals for determining heresy.

Most Cathari *parfaits* and *parfaites* (male and female clergy) leave their villages and take refuge in castles of sympathetic landowners such as Raimond de Pereille at Montségur, the fortress which becomes the Cathari citadel.

1230 Pope Gregory IX lifts the excommunication of Friedrich II temporarily settling their dispute.

1231 Pope Gregory IX declares that only he may decide who is and who is not a heretic and that the most appropriate punishment for heretics is to be burned at the stake.

1232 Pope Gregory IX establishes the Holy Roman Inquisition to rid the world of non-Catholic influences, including all Jewish and Muslim knowledge not part of Catholic orthodoxy. The Inquisition specifically prohibits <u>Bible</u> reading by laypersons; assumes guilt until proven innocent; and extends guilt for heresy to friends and family of the accused (in part to acquire their property, a privilege accorded to Inquisitors when a suspect is found guilty). Run primarily by Dominican and Franciscan monks, the Inquisition is a separate tribunal answerable only to the Papacy.

Upon the death of Pedro de Montaigu, Armand de Perigord becomes the 16th Templar Grand Master.

Pope Gregory IX assembles over 30,000 crusaders to attack the Cathari by promising extensive indulgences, eternal salvation, and the lands of the conquered. Many Templars refuse to take part and offer some Cathari refuge or accept fleeing Cathari into the Templars as brothers.

1235 In November, the people of Toulouse run Catholic Inquisitors out of town, angered by their extreme actions including exhumations to burn suspected very dead heretics.

1236 Catholic forces take Cordoba in Spain from the Muslims.

1238 Creation of an Augustinian monastery at Inchmahome in Scotland by the Earl of Monteith.

1239 Pope Gregory IX excommunicates Holy Roman Emperor Friedrich II a third time for denying Jesus' virgin birth.

On May 29, Inquisitor Robert le Bougre burns 183 Cathari at the stake at Montwimer (Marne) in France. Their protector, Catholic Bishop Moranis, is killed with them.

The Muslim Prince of Kerak conquers Jerusalem when the 1229 treaty expires.

1240 Holy Roman Emperor Friedrich II begins construction of Castel Del Monte 55km from Bari in Italy. This octagonal building is one of most unusual in the world.

Templars successfully attack Nablus.

Death of Muhyi'l-din Ibn al-Arabi, Sufi Saint (1165-1240), who traveled extensively in Europe, Africa, and the Middle East. His extensive writings of over 400 works focused on Hermetic interpretations of God. "To say that Christ is God is true in the sense that everything else is God, and to say that the Son of Mary is God is also true, but to say that God is Christ the son of Mary is false, because this would imply that He is Christ and nothing else. God is you and I and everything else in the universe." -- Muhyi'l-din Ibn al-Arabi

1241 Celestine IV becomes Pope after an arduous election process; he dies just 17 days later and the Papacy will be vacant for the two years.

Christians retake Jerusalem through negotiations led by the Hospitallers.

1242 In April, Cathari under Count Raimond VII de Toulouse and Pierre-Roger de Mirepoix kill ten Catholic Inquisitors. The murders provide the Pope with justification to launch another large-scale attack on the south of France.

1243   The Council of Beziers decides to lay siege to the Cathari fortress at Montségur, which begins on May 13. During the summer and winter, many Catholic soldiers defect to the Cathari.

On December 2, hoping to recruit him to finally crush the Cathari, Pope Innocent IV grants Count Raimond VII de Toulouse absolution for his rebellion in 1242.

1244   In January, four Cathari *parfaits*, Amiel Aicart, Hugues Paytavi, Pierre Bonet, and Mathieu, escape Montségur with Cathari artifacts, taking them first to fortified caves near Ussat, then to a castle at Montreal-de-Sos or Usson.

On March 1, about 340 Cathari at Montségur under the command of Pierre-Roger de Mirepoix agree to surrender in two weeks, giving them time to make peace with God.

On March 14, 200-225 Cathari at Montségur come down from the mountain and choose to burn at the stake rather than convert.

On July 11, the Sultan of Cairo's Turkish mercenaries under Pasha Khwarazmi retake Jerusalem, slaughtering many Catholics. Muslims divide into factions over the incident, with northern Muslims allying with the Catholics, and southern Muslims with the Sultan. On October 17, the two alliances meet in battle at Gaza and the Sultan's forces win, killing Templar Grand Master Armand de Perigord.

The Council of Narbonne declares that no leniency be allowed in the Holy Roman Inquisition. Sentences are to be harsh and may include the children and parents of those accused.

1245 Pope Innocent IV grants Inquisitors impunity: the authority to absolve themselves and their assistants from any acts of violence while carrying out their duties.

On July 27, the Council of Lyons (13th Ecumenical) Pope Innocent IV presides with King Baudouin, Eastern Emperor, and French King Louis IX (1214-1270). The council excommunicates (for the third time) and then deposes Holy Roman Emperor Friedrich II for attempting to make the Church part of government. The Council calls for a 7th Crusade against the Muslims and Mongols under the command of King Louis IX.

Richard de Bures becomes the 17th Templar Grand Master.

1246 According to <u>The Jesus Conspiracy</u>, King Louis IX sends two Dominican monks to Constantinople, knowing Eastern Emperor Baldwin II is short of funds and willing to sell relics of Jesus (crown of thorns, pieces of the True Cross) from the collection of Constantine's mother Helena from 900 years earlier. These relics include a *sancta toella tabule inserta* (holy towel mounted in a panel) – probably the item that will become known as the Shroud of Turin.

1247 On May 9, Richard de Bures dies and William de Sonnac becomes the 18th Templar Grand Master.

1248 King Louis IX's two Dominican monks return from Constantinople with unspecified relics of Jesus and place them on an island on the Seine at the Shrine of Sainte-Chapelle (near Notre Dame). They relics disappear during the French Revolution.

1250   At the Battle of Mansourah, Templar Grand Master William de Sonnac dies. Reynald de Vichiers (dies 1256) becomes the 19th Templar Grand Master.

On April 7, Muslims capture King Louis IX and his entire army. The crusade against Egypt fails. Ransomed by the Templars, King Louis IX and his major barons stay in Palestine and begin a major reconstruction campaign at Templar fortresses.

1252   Pope Innocent IV in *Ad extirpanda* authorizes the use of torture to encourage confessions as long as it does not result in mutilation or death.

Reynald de Vichiers' unapproved peace treaty with Damascus brings trouble with King Louis IX who banishes him from the Holy Land.

Thomas Berard takes over as the 20th Templar Grand Master.

English King Henry III accuses the Templars of excessive pride.

1254   King Louis IX leaves Castle Pilgrim in April.

1256   Pope Alexander IV (dies 1261) founds the Order of Augustine Hermits.

Last stand of the Cathari at Queribus, a fortress in southern France.

Mongols (a.k.a. Tartars) burn the library of the Order of Assassins at Alamut.

1258   Mongols destroy Baghdad and its 36 extensive libraries, including the 10,000-volume library of Vizir Ibn al-Alkami.

1259 Emergence of the Flagellants in southern Germany and northern Italy. Flagellants believe in self-punishment for sins by marching through the streets naked except for loincloths, whipping themselves, and crying to God for mercy. They believe sure salvation comes to all that stick to this practice for a thirty-three day period.

1260 Approximate founding of the Apostolici (a.k.a. Apostolic Brethren) by Gerard Segarelli (dies 1300). Apostolici believe that material possessions spoil the soul. They refuse to participate in any accumulation of materials goods, even clothes and food. Everything is in the moment, not the past nor the future. Despised by the Catholic hierarchy, they are frequently burned at the stake as heretics.

Mamalukes defeat the Mongols at Nazareth.

Templars build Castle Beaufort in Lebanon.

1261 Mamalukes continue their conquest of the Holy Land through defeating Christians in several locations.

1262 Pope Urban IV (1200~1264) grants Catholic Inquisitors the authority to absolve themselves and their assistants from any liability when those they torture die.

King Jayme I of Aragon orders the destruction of all Jewish texts.

1263 Birth of Roseline de Villeneuve (dies 1329), daughter of noted Catalan mystic and alchemist Arnaud de Villeneuve (1240~1311) and Sibylle de Sabran. Courageous and resourceful, she is known for a dramatic rescue of her crusader brother Helios from prison on Rhodes. Her feast day is January 17.

1265   Baybars the Conqueror, Sultan of Egypt, takes the Hospitaller fortress of Arsuf.

Pope Clement IV admonishes the Templars on their arrogance.

1266   According to *Holy Blood, Holy Grail*, Guillaume de Gisors (1219-1307) becomes Grand Master of the Prieuré de Sion.

Baybars the Conqueror takes the Templar strongholds of Castel Blanco and Castel Saphet (a.k.a. Safed). After victory at Safed, he gruesomely rings the Castel with severed Templar heads.

1267   According to the journals of Inquisitor Bernardo Gui, Charles the future King of Sicily, nephew of the King Louis XI, is present at the solemn expositions of the few fragments of relics of Mary Magdalene at Vézelay.

Baybars the Conqueror takes Jaffa, Antioch, Bagras, Sidon, Home, Belfort, and Tripoli.

1268   On May 18, Baybars the Conqueror captures Antioch. All of Palestine is under his control until Edward, Prince of Wales, invades by sea and pushes Baybars' troops back to Egypt. Edward and the Sultan sign a ten-year truce.

1270   On July 1, King Louis IX launches the 8th crusade. On August 27, King Louis IX and most of his army die from the plague in Tunisia. Philip III (born 1245) succeeds him as King of France.

1271   The Languedoc area of France, formerly home to the Cathari and other non-Christian groups, passes into control of King Philip III. The remaining Cathari communities are wiped out.

King Edward of England reaches a truce with Baybars the Conqueror.

1273 Establishment of a school in Spain specializing in the Kabbala and alchemy.

In March, Templar Grand Master Thomas Berard dies. In May, Guillaume de Beaujeu becomes the 21st Grand Master.

Death of Djelaleddin Rumi (a.k.a. Maulavi, born 1207), Persian poet, Sufi Saint, and founder of the Order of the Whirling Dervishes. "The lamps are many but the light is one." - Rumi

1274 In January, the 2nd Council of Lyon (14th Ecumenical) under Pope Gregory X (a.k.a, Tedaldo Visconti, 1210-1276) and Holy Roman Emperor Rudolph I temporarily reunite Catholicism with the Eastern Orthodox Church. It reaffirms the Council of 381 and lays down rules for papal elections, including a secret ballot. Pope Gregory X suggests the Templars and the Hospitallers merge which both groups successfully oppose. The Council also chastises but does not condemn Thomas Aquinas and forbids new monastic orders.

Thomas Aquinas (born 1225), Catholic theologian and Benedictine monk, writes to reconcile God and Man in a unity of thought. His book *Summa Theologica* superbly compiles comprehensive statements of Catholic doctrine. He dies several months after his appearance at the Council of Lyons.

1276 Three different Popes serve during this year due to a series of untimely deaths: Innocent V (1224-1276), Hadrian V (1205-1276), and John XXI (1215-1277).

1277 Pope Nicholas III (1215-1280) exiles Franciscan scholar and scientist Roger Bacon for heresy until 1292.

1279 On December 9, Future King of Sicily and Count de Provence Charles II excavates the crypt at Saint Maximin le Sainte-Baume, France in search of the body and relics of Mary Magdalene. He declares a positive identification of her body can be made (from the many bodies buried there) by a divine odor and by a patch of pink skin where Jesus touched her at his resurrection.

1280 Abraham Abulafia (1240-1292), a leading Kabbalist from Spain, publicly sets off for Rome to convert Pope Nicholas III to Judaism. Abulafia spends long hours in meditation and works with the Hebrew alphabet to create new meaningful names for God. Fortunately for Abulafia, whose arrival (and execution) is anticipated in Rome, the Pope dies the day before and the execution is canceled.

Death of Albertus Magnus (born 1193), the foremost Western Kabbalist and Hermeticist of the medieval era. Theologian, Dominican monk, philosopher, and alchemist, his expertise included botany, astronomy, physics, geology, and a synthesis between Catholic and Hermetic thought.

1282 Templars under Guillaume de Beaujeu sign a treaty with Sultan Qalawun (a.k.a. al-Malik al-Mansur) guaranteeing the safety of their castle at Tortosa in return for their promise not to attack the Sultan for 10 years.

1283 The German Hospitallers become the Teutonic Knights and complete conquering Prussia, establishing a homeland they call the Ordensland. Catholics accuse them of witchcraft but their remote locations in Prussia and the Baltic Coast place them safely beyond authority.

1284 Philippe IV (1268-1314), son of Philippe III and grandson of King Louis IX, marries Jeanne of Navarre (1271-1305) on August 16. He becomes ruler of Navarre until her death. Known for his light hair and good looks, he is called "le bel" (the fair).

1285 Council of Constantinople.

French King Philippe III dies in October.

1286 On January 6, Philippe IV becomes King of France at Reims. His reign will be known for its greed. Philippe IV will tax and seize the property of Jews and Lombards, tax the population including the clergy, debase the currency, and vilify the Templars.

1288 Glasses are invented to improve vision but their worldly powers are viewed by many as the work of the devil.

1290 King Edward I of England expels the country's Jews.

1291 On April 5, the Mameluke Muslims under al-Ashraf besiege the Catholics at Acre.

On May 18, Mameluke Muslims significantly undermine Acre. William de Beaujeu dies defending Acre and that night. Tibald de Gaudin sails for Sidon with the Templar treasury and relics. At Sidon, Tibald de Gaudin becomes the 22nd Templar Grand Master. When Sidon falls, Templars take their archives to Tortosa then to Cyprus before a final voyage to Venice then France.

On May 28, Mameluke Muslims take Acre. This is the end of Christian control of the Holy Land.

On August 3, Templars evacuate their castle at Tortosa. On August 14, Templars evacuate Castle Pilgrim. Some move to the tiny island of Ruad, off Tortosa. This defeat loses the Holy Land for Catholics until the time of Napoleon.

The Dominicans and Franciscans launch an Inquisition against the Bogomils in Bulgaria.

1293   On April 16, Tibald Gaudin dies and Jacques de Molay (1244-1314) becomes the 23rd Templar Grand Master.

1294   Five-month term of Pope Celestine V (1209-1296). Prior to becoming Pope, he established the Franciscan Order of the Celestines (a.k.a. Hermits of Murrone). But as Pope, he becomes increasingly unhappy in the office to which he had been unwillingly elected. Aide Bishop Benedict Gatano (1235-1303) plays on Celestine's insecurity to persuade him to resign, the first pope to do so.

Gatano becomes Pope Boniface VIII and imprisons the former Pope in the Castle Fumone until Celestine's death in 1296.

1295   King of Sicily Charles II begins construction on a large cathedral on the site of Mary Magdalene's crypt at Baume.

Scotland and France declare a mutual defense treaty.

1296   Dominican Inquisitors turn their attention to the Franciscans, their own spiritual brothers, as heretics.

England annexes Scotland and removes Scotland's Coronation Stone, the "Stone of Destiny," to Westminster Abbey.

England expels its Jews.

Pope Boniface VIII excommunicates King Philippe IV for asserting the right to tax the clergy. They reconcile the following year, with the Pope capitulating fearing the complete loss of French revenues.

Chapter Five: Downfall

Despite their worldly success, the shine is less bright on the Templars' reputation. Having lost the Holy Land completely, including most of their military facilities, they retreat to Europe to a central banking role. Yet they will become victims of jealousy over their incredible wealth and power. Soon, they will really anger the wrong person, the arrogant expansionist French King Philippe IV. Reeling from various military defeats, failed domestic programs, and increasing unpopularity, he blames the Templars and campaigns to cement that belief with the public and the powerful.

1297 Financed in part through Templar loans, King Philippe IV attacks various areas in Europe with mixed success.

A Scottish army under the command of William Wallace and Sir William Sinclair defeats English King Edward's 30,000-man army at the Battle of Stirling Bridge.

1301 The young Louis IV becomes King of Bavaria.

1302 Pope Boniface VIII prevents King Philippe IV from collecting taxes from the French Church. Philippe closes the borders to the export of money or materials to the Vatican and begins a smear campaign against the Pope. These actions result in Philippe's excommunication and the issuance of the Unam Sanctum, an edict which requires complete submission to the Papacy, saying "We declare, we say, we defend and pronounce that to every human creature it is absolutely necessary to salvation to be subject to the Roman Pontiff."

After many casualties, Templars leave Ruad for good and travel to Cyprus.

King Edward of England seizes the Templar treasury in London and offers to give it to the poor. Pope Boniface intervenes and Edward returns the money. Undaunted, and with unpaid troops from previous military campaigns wanting to be paid, he enters the London Temple on false pretenses and robs it again.

1303 In September, King Philippe IV's advisor, the Cathari Guillaume de Nogaret (dies 1314), storms the Papal home in Anagni and violently threatens Pope Boniface VIII, who dies of the stress five weeks later. His successor, Pope Benedict XI (a.k.a. Niccolo Boccasini, 1240-1304), is at first conciliatory but later excommunicates de Nogaret.

The English and the Scots fight at Roslin, a battle won by the Scots with the help of Templar knights.

1304	The anti-clerical Dolcinites, in rebellion against a wealthy Church, wipe out entire Catholic towns, kill priests, and make many enemies. Their leader Friar Dolcino of Novara zealously believes in the holiness of poverty.
	On July 7, Pope Benedict XI dies, many believe from poisoning by Guillaume de Nogaret.
1305	Death of King Philippe IV's wife, Jeanne of Navarre, sister of the Count of Champagne. King Philippe IV's various military campaigns take a huge financial toll on his treasury. When his wife dies he applies for membership in the Templars, offering to abdicate to his son in return. Templars insist he pay off substantially overdue debt first, which he refuses.
	In November, King Philippe IV installs Pope Clement V (1260-1329, a.k.a. Bertrand de Goth), whose mother is Ida de Blanchefort of the family of Bertrand de Blanchefort, 6th Templar Grand Master.
1306	In February, Pope Clement V excommunicates Robert the Bruce (1275-1329) for the murder of John Comyn, Robert's rival for the Scottish throne.
	A large group of Ethiopian representatives meets with Pope Clement V in Avignon.
	The Countess of Buchan crowns Robert the Bruce King of Scotland at Scone.
	In June, King Philippe IV devalues the French currency and has to take refuge from angry mobs inside the Paris Templar preceptory.
	Templars help overthrow King Henry II on Cyprus and Amaury de Lusignan takes over.

On July 21, to raise funds, King Philippe IV orders the arrest and expulsion of all Jews in France and takes their property, for which the Templars publicly criticize him.

The Hospitallers, under the command of Grand Master William de Villaret, conquer the island of Rhodes from the Byzantine Emperor and change their name to the Knights of Rhodes.

1307 Bernardo Gui (1261-1331) becomes the Catholic Inquisitor for Toulouse until 1323. After great success oppressing Cathari, he moves to Paris to torture Templars.

According to <u>Holy Blood, Holy Grail,</u> Edouard de Bar becomes Grand Master of the Prieuré de Sion.

On March 23, Pope Clement V arrests and executes Dolcinite Friar Dolcino in Novara.

Pope Clement V calls a meeting with Templar Grand Master Jacques de Molay and Knights of Rhodes Grand Master William de Villaret about merging their orders and reporting to King Philippe IV. William de Villaret cannot attend but de Molay sails to La Rochelle from Cyprus (with eighteen Templar ships). Once in France, he meets in Paris with King Philippe IV.

In May, de Molay and King Philippe IV travel to meet with Pope Clement V in Poitiers. De Molay defends himself against charges of heretical practices and declines request to merge the Templars with the Hospitallers and place both under King Philippe IV.

In August, Jacques de Molay meets with the Pope for a second time and asks him to intervene against King Philippe IV's propaganda campaign against the Templars.

On September 14, King Phillippe IV secretly orders the arrest of all Templars.

On Friday, October 13, King Philippe IV orders the arrest of all Templars within his jurisdiction on charges of secret rituals, non-Catholic beliefs, homosexuality, and teaching abortion to women, worshipping idols, disrespecting the cross, and associating with Jews and Muslims. The King's forces find only 620 of an estimated 3000 Templars. Those captured include Grand Master Jacques de Molay, Hughes de Peyraud, and Geoffroi de Charnay (1248-1314), Preceptor of Normandy. Both are tortured and possibly (briefly) crucified. De Molay confesses to denying the divinity of Jesus but claims innocence on other charges. He and de Charnay go to prison.

The treasury of the Templars' Paris preceptory disappears prior to the arrival of Philippe IV's forces. Where did it go? Eighteen Templar ships based in La Rochelle on the coast of France disappear, suggesting the treasury was moved from the country. According to Andrew Sinclair in Sword and the Grail, French Masonic tradition places nine Templar ships at the Isle of Mey near Edinburgh. According to Baigent and Leigh in The Temple and the Lodge, ships of the Templar fleet sail around Ireland to land in the Argyll area of Scotland -- where they are warmly received. However, according to Karen Ralls in The Templars and the Grail, "we have no concrete evidence that a number of ships left La Rochelle in 1307 after the arrests." Ralls proposes that any escape by sea would have been from Aragon, a port under greater Templar control than La Rochelle.

Hearings on the Templars begin in Paris on October 19. Under torture, Jacques de Molay confesses on October 24. On October 27, Pope Clement V orders the arrest of all remaining Templars. On November 9, Hughes de Peyraud confesses.

On December 24, de Molay and other Templar leaders withdraw their confessions.

1308　In January, King Edward II arrests Templars in England and imprisons the English Grand Master. Like his father, he robs the treasury at the London Temple.

In February, Pope Clement V suspends the Inquisition against the Templars for a month.

In May, Templars on Cyprus surrender to the Order-friendly King Amaury de Lusignan and proclaim their innocence.

On May 26, King Phillippe IV visits Pope Clement V at Poitiers, threatening the Pope to more fully condemn the Templars.

Pope Clement V issues <u>Regnas in Coelis,</u> which orders the leaders of all Catholic lands to investigate the Templars.

On June 27, King Phillippe IV sends Pope Clement V 72 handpicked Templars to confess personally.

Between the 17th and 20th of July, Cardinals interview Jacques de Molay, Geoffroi de Charnay, and Hughes de Peyraud in Chinon Castle. Under torture, the prisoners decide to reinstate their confessions denying the divinity of Jesus. Their geometrical carvings on the walls of the prison tower still exist but have never been deciphered.

In August, Pope Clement V moves from Rome to the Dominican monastery at Avignon. Over the next 70 years, Avignon will become known as a center of religion -- and prostitution. Avignon's brothel industry booms and entrepreneurs such as Johanna of Naples have thriving businesses. Johanna eventually sells to Pope Clement VI who keeps it going under the name The Abbey.

Many Templars are massacred at St-Martin-de-Vesubie.

The Knights Templar Chronology

1309   On August 8, the Paris Commission begins hearings in Vienneto more objectively investigate charges against the Templars.

On November 26, de Molay and others are made to appear at the Paris Commission.

1310   On March 28, imprisoned Templars in Poitiers request an audience with Pope Clement V, which King Philippe IV refuses.

On April 7, the Paris Commission brings 127 charges against the Templars in seven categories:

- Denying the divinity of Jesus
- Worshipping a head with magical powers
- Disbelieving in the Catholic sacraments
- Receiving confessions without being official priests
- Conducting homosexual-oriented acts
- Being materially oriented
- Having secret meetings and rituals

King Henry II retakes power in Cyprus and retaliates against the Templars, destroying their castles and removing official protections against their persecution.

Under direction from King Philippe IV, Archbishop of Sens Philip de Marigny, brother of the King's finance minister, convenes the Council of Sens, asserts authority over the Templar trials, and burns 54-120 Templar prisoners on May 12.

In Salamanca, Spain, King Dinis I declares the Templars innocent in Iberian territory.

1311　In May, after a year of discussions, the Paris Commission finds the Templars innocent, although many Templars admit to some degree of the beliefs charged against them, such as that Jesus was a man and not a God.

On October 16, Pope Clement V convenes the Council of Viennes (15th Ecumenical) along with King Philippe IV of France, King Edward II of England, and King James II of Aragon. Impatient to get the Templar riches, Philippe IV pushes the slow-moving Council to be tougher. The Council declares anyone who believes that "the rational or intellectual soul is not the form of the human body in itself and essentially, must be regarded as a heretic." Beside the Templars, the Council condemns the Beghards and the Beguines, although treatment of the female Beguines is much more lenient.

1312　In March, Pope Clement V's _Vox in excelso_ and _Ad Providam_ officially dissolve the Templars and transfers their property except for lands in Spain to the Knights Hospitallers.

1313　Pope Clement V declares Pope Celestine V a Saint.

1314　On March 14, Philippe orders the execution of Templars Jacques de Molay, Geoffroi de Charnay (Grand Preceptor of Normandy), Hugh de Peyraud (Visitor-General), and Guy d'Auvergne (Grand Preceptor of France).

On March 18, Jacques de Molay and Geoffroi de Charnay are scheduled to burn at the stake in Paris on the Ile des Javiaux on the Seine River. Hugh de Peyraud and Guy d'Auvergne confess and get life imprisonment. Fear crowd reprisals against them from passionate speeches from de Molay and de Charnay, authorities delay their execution.

A few hours later, Philippe IV has de Molay and de Charnay burned privately near the convent of St. Augustine.

Legend has it that a man in the crowd curses all those associated with the executions to death within a year. On April 20, Pope Clement V dies. On November 29, King Philippe IV dies in a hunting accident. The "curse" is fulfilled.

On June 24, Scottish troops led by Robert the Bruce and Sir Henry Sinclair defeat the English at the Battle of Bannockburn, making Scotland an independent nation. Legend has it that Templars fleeing persecution in France assist the Scots in their victory.

1315 Death of Ramon Lull of Mallorca, Spain (born 1229), expert in Sufi, Hermetic, and Kabalistic thought.

Excommunication of the Fraticelli, purist Dominicans who uphold Francis' ideals of poverty. Pope Clement V destroys their settlement at Magnalata and has everyone there killed.

1316 Pope John XXII (a.k.a, Jacques d'Euse, 1244-1334) sends eight Dominican monks to Ethiopia to search for the mythic emperor Prester John.

1317 On December 30, Pope John XXII in *Sancta Romana* declares the Bizochi, the Fraticelli, and the Spirituals (a.k.a. Zelanti) as heretics. Spirituals are Franciscan monks who believe in the spiritual purity of poverty to the point that it threatens the Papacy and its immense wealth. They believe Jesus owned no property, and therefore the church should also be poor. Those who refuse to submit to Papal authority are to be burned at the stake. He also bans the study and practice of alchemy.

Founding of the Order of Montesa, a special order of Spanish knights set up to receive former Templars fleeing from French persecution.

1319 On March 14, Pope John XXII in *Ad ea exquibis* approves the Knights of Christ, a chivalric order based in the former Templar stronghold of Tomar, Portugal. Founder King Dinis I of Portugal (1279-1325) recruits former Templars from France and ingeniously "seizes" Templar properties in Portugal for the new order. Members will include Vasco de Gama (1462-1524), King Alphonso IV, and Prince Henry the Navigator (1394-1460), with their ships bearing the red Templar *patte* cross. Gil Martins becomes the first Grand Master and the order expands to 69 knights by 1321.

1320 Sir Henry St. Clair along with other Scottish noblemen signs the Declaration of Arbroath, a petition to Pope John XXII to officially recognize Scottish independence from England. The petition is successful, and the Pope signs.

Pope John XXII authorizes the Inquisition to prosecute sorcery.

Inquisitor Bernardo Gui publishes manuals and procedures for Inquisitors called the *Practica Inquisitionis.*

1321 Belibaste, one of the last known Cathari priests or *parfaits* in southern France, is burned at the stake.

1323 England recognizes Scotland as an independent nation in the Treaty of Northampton and arranges the marriage of Robert the Bruce's son David to Joanna, the daughter of Edward II.

Pope John XXII asks King Louis IV of Bavaria (dies 1347) to abdicate his throne.

1324   On May 22, King Louis IV of Bavaria accuses Pope John XXII in the *Sachsenhausen Appellation* of heresy for his proclamations against ecclesiastical poverty.

1326   Pope John XXII in *Super illius specula* declares it heresy to say that Jesus and the apostles owned no property, justifying Catholic wealth since it violates no sacred principle. The Pope also declares any deliberate contact with spirits to be heresy, opening the door for new inquisitions on witchcraft.

1327   Death of Meister Eckhart von Hocheim (born 1327), a German Dominican mystic who led the Brethren of the Free Spirit (a.k.a. Friends of God). He questioned the need for a church, believing that when individuals are directly connected with God no further organization is necessary. They believe every created thing is divine, and that the place to look for God is within oneself.

Setting of Umberto Eco's novel The Name of the Rose, a murder mystery set in remote monastery during meetings between Franciscan and Dominican monks on whether the Church should be poor.

1328   Pope John XXII excommunicates William of Ockham (1285-1349), brilliant Franciscan monk, for his writings on papal fallibility, logic, and the civil authority of the church. Against the circular and complex arguments of Catholic logic on faith, he used a principle later named for him -- Occam's Razor -- which may be stated as "A plurality (of reasons) should not be posited without necessity" or "Among many complex explanations, the simplest is usually right."

King Louis IV of Bavaria crowned as Holy Roman Emperor.

1329   Robert the Bruce dies June 7 of leprosy. His dying wish was to go to Jerusalem to fight the Muslims.

Pope John XXII undoes the excommunication of Robert The Bruce and accepts his successors as Kings of Scotland. He also condemns Meister Eckhart as a heretic.

1330   Sir William Sinclair (born 1297), his brother John Sinclair, Sir James Douglas, and Sir Robert Keith, take the embalmed heart of Robert the Bruce to Jerusalem. In Spain, under Muslim attack, they lose the heart. All die in battle but Keith, who later recovers it and returns it to Melrose Abbey in Scotland.

Death of Ubertino of Casale (born 1259), a brilliant Franciscan monk who passionately believes in the poverty of Jesus, a view for which he is held in contempt, especially after the Papal edict of 1326.

1333   The "Black Death," a plague which begins in China, spreads via trade routes throughout Europe killing 27-40 million people. Although originating from a Mongol attack on a trading post in the Crimea, the public places blame for the plague on heretics, Jews, and Muslims. The huge surplus of clothes and bed linens left by the dead creates a new industry -- rag paper.

1334   On December 4, Pope John XXII dies.

1335   Pope Benedict XII (1280-1342), a former inquisitor of the Cathari and Waldensians, issues new orders for the reform of monks.

In Toulouse, Catholic Inquisitors extract confessions of witchcraft by torturing 63 people, including Anna-Marie de Georgei, accused of attending a "witches sabbath."

1336   According to <u>Holy Blood, Holy Grail</u>, Jeanne de Bar becomes Grand Master of the Prieuré de Sion.

1338   In the Declaration of Rense, Holy Roman Emperor Louis IV declares that imperial authority comes directly from God and does not require Papal approval.

1347   Death of Holy Roman Emperor Louis IV.

1349   Pope Clement VI (1291-1352) condemns the Flagellants.

1350   Francesco Petrarch (1304-1374) and Giovanni Boccacio (1313-1376) travel to various monasteries in search of ancient Greek and Roman texts. With the help of Leonzio Pilato, they obtain copies of the Iliad and the Odyssey in Byzantium and translate them into Latin for the first time.

1351   According to Holy Blood, Holy Grail, Jean de St. Clair becomes Grand Master of the Prieuré de Sion.

1357   According to Knight and Lomas in The Hiram Key and The Second Messiah, the Shroud resurfaces and goes on public display at Livey, lent by Jeanne de Vergy, the widow of Geoffroi de Charnay (dies 1356). This Geoffroi is grandson of the brother of Geoffroi de Charnay who died alongside Jacques de Molay. After complaints by the Bishop of Troyes Pierre d'Arcis, Jeanne de Vergy stops showing the shroud and it is placed into hiding.

1362   Urban V takes over as Pope.

1366   Prince Henry Sinclair (1345-1400), Lord of Rosslyn, leads a group of Scottish knights to help King Peter I of Cyprus successfully attack Egypt at Alexandria. Upon his return to Scotland, he marries Janet Halyburton.

   According to Holy Blood, Holy Grail, Blanche d'Evreaux becomes Grand Master of the Prieuré de Sion.

1377   On January 17, Pope Gregory XI (1329-1378), under the influence of Catherine of Siena (1347-1380), returns the papacy to Rome from Avignon. He disciplines the Knights Hospitallers and condemns Catholic reformer John Wyclif (born 1328).

Catholic forces under Robert of Geneva (later Pope Clement VII) kill between 2,500 and 5,000 people in Cessna, Italy, for rebelling against Papal control.

1378   Upon Pope Gregory XI's death, two Popes claim power, Pope Urban VI (1318-1389) in Rome and Pope Clement VII at Avignon.

1379   King Haakon of Norway installs Prince Henry Sinclair as Earl of Orkney and Lord of the Shetland Islands.

1380   John Wyclif (1320-1384), an Oxford theologian, translates the <u>Bible</u> completely into old English. He includes a prologue that preaches against the abuses of the Papacy, the improper veneration of relics, transubstantiation as a false miracle, and the false power of the Pope (for Wyclif, there is no human spokesperson for God). Pope Urban VI predictably condemns him and his followers, the Lollards.

1389   The Shroud goes back on public display in Lirey until 1398, when it is again hidden until 1453.

1390   Italian navigator Nicolo Zeno travels to the Orkneys to join Prince Henry Sinclair as he prepares to mount and transatlantic journey to a new world -- North America.

1392   Nicolo Zeno and Prince Henry Sinclair receive permission from English King Richard II to travel to London and obtain three ships for their transatlantic exploration.

1393	Sinclair sends Nicolo Zeno and three ships on a survey mission to find a route to the North America. On the way, Zeno discovers an Augustian monastery in Greenland, St. Olaf's, at Unartoq on Gael Hamke Bay. There, hot springs and abundant fishing make a high quality of life.
1395	Nicolo Zeno returns to the Orkneys with extensive mapping of Greenland. He dies shortly thereafter of exposure and Sinclair replaces him with his Antonio Zeno, fresh into town with new Italian galleys and cannons.
1398 See Map 7.	In May, Prince Henry Sinclair, Sir James Gunn, Antonio Zeno, and crew leave the Orkney Islands with 12 ships for a full expedition to the North American mainland. Sinclair lands in Nova Scotia (near Louisburg) and the indigenous Micmacs indians welcome the explorers as "White Gods" and Sinclair as "Glooscap." In stark contrast to other explorers, especially the Spanish, Sinclair promotes trade, fishing, and farming over violence and conquest. Sinclair sails to what will become Newport, Rhode Island. There he builds a stone tower as church, lighthouse, and observatory patterned after the Sinclair Church at Corstorphine. Later in the voyage, Sinclair's officer Sir James Gunn dies and Sinclair buries him in what would later be Westford, Massachusetts. You can see what is claimed to me his tombstone there still. According to <u>Holy Blood, Holy Grail,</u> alchemist Nicholas Flamel becomes Grand Master of the Prieuré de Sion.
1400	Prince Henry Sinclair returns to the Orkneys, the first European to have discovered America. He finds himself immediately enmeshed in a trade war and is killed by the Hansa (a.k.a. the Hanseatic League), German merchants seeking control of the North Sea shipping business.
1492	Christopher Columbus reaches North America.

Modern orders claim direct lineage to the Knights Templar. They claim that some Templars escaped France with long-guarded documents and vast treasure; that these Templars assimilated into a native European population but continued to hide their records and treasure; that a new brotherhood sprung directly from the Templars and continues to this day, partially public, partially secret. Those claims may be true, but they are as yet unsubstantiated. We do know that while many groups from the Masons to the Rosicrucians borrow liberally from Templar rituals, beliefs, values, symbols, roles, titles, and structures, there is no evidence yet of any *direct* succession.

Bibliography

1972 British film producer Henry Lincoln shoots the first of three documentaries on Rennes-le-Château for the BBC, <u>The Lost Treasure of Jerusalem</u>. For the first time, the story of this small French town's parish priest, Berenger Saunière, and his sudden wealth reaches a large audience.

1974 Henry Lincoln produces <u>The Priest, The Painter, and the Devil</u>, his second on Rennes-le-Château.

1978 Professor Malcolm Barber writes <u>The Trial of the Templars</u> about the suppression of the Templars in France.

1979 Jean-Luc Chaumeil writes <u>Le Trésor du Triangle d'Or</u>, an accounting of the parchments allegedly found at Rennes-le-Château concerning the existence of the Prieuré de Sion, a group dedicated over the course of centuries to the return of a Jesus-based bloodline to government and the Papacy. Baigent, Lincoln, and Leigh will base <u>Holy Blood, Holy Grail</u> on these documents. According to Chaumeil, the parchments are forgeries cooked up by two men, Pierre Plantard and Marquis Philippe de Chérisey.

Henry Lincoln produces <u>The Shadow of the Templars</u>, his third documentary.

1981 On August 21, Muslims in Jerusalem barricade themselves inside an ancient Templar-dug tunnel at the Temple Mount opened by Israeli authorities. Eight days later, Muslims seal the tunnel with concrete fearing an Israeli incursion all the way under the sacred Dome of the Rock.

1982 Producer Henry Lincoln teams with Michael Baigent (born 1948) and Richard Leigh, to publish the blockbuster Holy Blood, Holy Grail. They investigate the Templars' alleged involvement in keeping great "secrets" over hundreds of years. The most controversial of these secrets: Jesus did not die on the cross but lived to marry Mary Magdalene and father children whose bloodline continues to this day.

Professor George A. Wells (born 1926) publishes The Historical Evidence for Jesus, arguing that Paul and the Gospel writers made up most of the information in the New Testament to politically advance their version of Christianity.

Stephen Howarth writes The Knights Templar.

1983 The Discovery of the Grail (a.k.a, The Eternity Machine, Die Entdeckung des Heiligen Grals) by brothers Johannes (1956-1999) and Peter Fiebag, explores a connection between the Templars and the Holy Grail, which in their opinion is an extraterrestrial machine. This machine, arriving here for reasons unknown, generated manna from a nuclear energy source to feed the people of Israel 3000 years ago. The authors suggest the Templars were guardians of this secret during their heyday and voyaged to Canada to ultimately bury the machine at Oak Island.

1984 Ian Wilson writes <u>Jesus: The Evidence</u>.

Stephen Knight (a.k.a., Swami Puja Debal, 1951-1985) writes <u>The Brotherhood</u>, with many sensational allegations about Masons, among them ties to the Soviet KGB.

Elizabeth Claire Prophet (born 1939), leader of the Church Universal and Triumphant (a.k.a. Summit Lighthouse), publishes <u>The Lost Years of Jesus</u> about his life between the ages of 12 and 30, based largely on the travels and writings of Nicolas Roerich about Jesus in Tibet.

1985 <u>The Cult of the Black Virgin</u> by former monk Ean Begg explores the meaning, veneration, and locations of Black Madonnas across Europe and their connection to Jesus, Mary, and Mary Magdalene.

Pierre Jarnac writes <u>Histoire du Trésor de Rennes-le-Château</u> featuring a 1974 letter from Phillippe de Chérisey confessing to forging the parchments.

Cardinal Joseph Ratzinger, closest advisor to the Pope, criticizes all reforms since Vatican II, stating "the freedom of the act of faith cannot justify a right to dissent."

1986 Death of Jidde Krishnamurti, Indian religious philosopher and former wunderkind of the Theosophical Society. His writings include The Urgency of Change and The Awakening of Intelligence. Krishnamurti believed that sorrow and conflict are the result of a conditioned mind and that to reduce sorrow one must change that conditioning.

Michael Baigent, Richard Leigh, and Henry Lincoln write The Messianic Legacy, an extension of Holy Blood Holy Grail, to explore Rennes-le-Château, the Prieuré de Sion, and the Jesus bloodline.

Edward Burman writes The Templars: Knights of God, based on documents from the British Library on Templar history.

Jean Markale writes The Templar Treasure at Gisors (a.k.a. Gisors et L'Enigme des Templiers), speculating that lost Templar treasure resides in the tunnel system beneath the former Templar castle at Gisors in France. He also writes Montségur and the Mystery of the Cathars (a.k.a. Montségur et L'Enigme Cathare).

Robert C. Walton writes the Chronological and Background Charts of Church History, a quick reference guide to religious groups.

The Duke of Edinburgh convenes a meeting of world religious leaders at Saint Francis' Basilica in Assisi, Italy. In an unusual show of religious unity, Pope John Paul II leads 100 world religious leaders (Catholic, Protestant) in prayers for peace. Also this year, Pope John Paul II becomes the first Pope known to visit a Jewish synagogue.

1988   Burton Mack publishes <u>A Myth of Innocence</u>, which holds that the Gospels contain very little historically authentic information about Jesus. Mack puts forward that Jesus was not with a divine being, but a wise, very human, sage. Mack believes that after Jesus' death his followers tried to keep the "countercultural" wisdom alive by attaching supernatural myths drawn from other belief systems familiar to Greco-Roman audiences.

Gerard de Sède (born 1921) writes <u>Rennes-le-Château</u> which admits the Chérisey documents were forged and that no Jesus bloodline exists today.

Umberto Eco publishes <u>Foucault's Pendulum</u>, a novel about a six-hundred-year-old conspiracy started by Templars surviving the end of their order.

Michael Baigent and Richard Leigh, in <u>The Temple and the Lodge,</u> trace Templars who escaped from Philip IV to Scotland and their subsequent development of Freemasonry.

Michael Anderson Bradley and Deanna Theilmann-Bean write <u>Holy Grail Across The Atlantic: The Secret History of Canadian Discovery and Exploration,</u> asserting that Prince Henry Sinclair hid treasure and artifacts in Oak Island's elaborate pit.

1989   Welsh author Michael Howard writes <u>The Occult Conspiracy,</u> tracing the occult influence of secret societies on politics and statecraft through the centuries from ancient Egypt to the present era, including the Templars and the Masons.

1990 John J. Robinson writes <u>Born In Blood: The Lost Secrets of Freemasonry</u>, a history of the Templars and their links to Freemasonry.

William Still writes <u>New World Order: The Ancient Plan of Secret Societies</u>, linking together various groups, including the Templars, with a vast conspiracy for world control.

Professor Peter Partner publishes <u>The Knights Templar and Their Myth</u> about facts and fabrications of the Order.

1991 John J. Robinson writes <u>Dungeon, Fire, and Sword</u>, a follow-up to <u>Born in Blood</u> about the early history of the Templars.

Bernard Grun and Daniel Boorstin publish <u>The Timetables of History</u>, an essential and comprehensive chronology of recorded events.

Henry Lincoln writes <u>The Holy Place</u> about Rennes-le-Château.

1992　Dr. Barbara Thiering publishes <u>Jesus and the Riddle of The Dead Sea Scrolls</u> (a.k.a. <u>Jesus the Man</u>), using the pesher technique to decipher the Gospels. Her scholarly but controversial research methods portray a Jesus who marries Mary Magdalene, survives the crucifixion, divorces Mary Magdalene, and remarries to a woman named Lydia when he is 57.

Michael Bradley writes <u>The Columbus Conspiracy: An Investigation into the Secret History of Christopher Columbus</u>, explaining the conspiracy to give Columbus credit for discovering an America that Bradley maintains Prince Henry Sinclair discovered almost 100 years earlier.

The Vatican again admits its error in charging Galileo with heresy.

In April, Niven Sinclair (born 1923) and Judith Fisken, Curator of Rosslyn Chapel, found the Friends of Rosslyn, a non-profit group dedicated to the Chapel's preservation and careful exploration.

Niven Sinclair obtains permission for ground scans and digging at Rosslyn Chapel. His cousin Andrew Sinclair publishes <u>The Sword and the Grail</u> about the connection between the Chapel, the Templars, and the Masons. Sinclair's book chronicles the exciting but unsuccessful excavation of the Chapel's crypt. While encouraged by massive stone blocks that indicate a true crypt system, the effort needed to go further without damaging the building brings digging to a halt. Other than a wooden bowl and a few small artifacts, the project reveals nothing.

Graham Hancock writes <u>The Sign and the Seal</u>, tracking theories about the Lost Ark of the Covenant in Ethiopia including the role of the Templars.

Reverend Lionel Fanthorpe and Patricia Fanthorpe write <u>Secrets of Rennes-le-Château</u>.

Henry Lincoln and Erling Haagensen make <u>The Secret</u>, a video about Rennes-le-Château and a geometric pattern of Templar churches on the Danish island of Bornholm. Shown later on the Discovery Channel as the <u>Secrets of the Templars</u>.

1993 The Friends of Rosslyn purchase Gardiner's Brae, land immediately adjacent and east of Rosslyn Chapel.

Robert W. Funk, Roy W. Hoover, and The Jesus Seminar publish <u>The Five Gospels: What Did Jesus Really Say?</u>, an analysis of the accuracy and likelihood, based on scholarship, history, and other sources, of statements attributed to Jesus in the <u>Bible</u>.

Helen Nicholson writes <u>Templars, Hospitallers, and Teutonic Knights: Images of the Military Orders 1128-1191</u>.

William Crooker writes <u>Oak Island Gold</u> on the history of Oak Island, Canada's most famous enigma.

Peter Partner writes <u>The Murdered Magicians: The Templars and their Myth</u>, a traditional history of the Order.

1994 Sufi Fida Hassnain (born 1924), retired Professor and Director of Archives, Archeology, Research and Museums, publishes <u>A Search for the Historical Jesus: From Apocryphal, Buddhist, Islamic, and Sanskrit Sources</u>, concluding from Buddhist, Islamic and Sanskrit sources that Jesus did not die on the Cross. Following the research of Nicholas Roerich and others in Tibet, he tracks legends of Jesus post-crucifixion to his actual death in Kashmir. According to Hassnain, "The religion of Buddha, of Moses, of Jesus and Mohammed, become one at a higher level."

In March, the Friends of Rosslyn bring in a French drilling crew and attempt to excavate Rosslyn Chapel's crypts sideways from Gardiner's Brae. Although the project is condoned by the Earl of Rosslyn, the Scottish government agency for historic preservation brings it to a halt, embarrassing everyone and heavily damaging relations between the Friends of Rosslyn and the Earl of Rosslyn.

Friends of Rosslyn publish The Templar Legacy & The Masonic Inheritance within Rosslyn Chapel, by Tim Wallace-Murphy and Michael Green, an attempt to interpret the symbolism of Rosslyn Chapel's carvings and windows.

Holger Kersten and Elmar Gruber write The Jesus Conspiracy: The Turin Shroud and the Truth about the Resurrection and Jesus Lived in India: His Unknown Life Before and After the Crucifixion.

Edward Burman writes Supremely Abominable Crimes: The Trial of the Knights Templar, a narrative of the Templars' trial in Paris.

Malcolm Barber writes The New Knighthood: A History of the Order of the Temple, exploring the reality and myth of the Templars. This includes a brief chronology of events related to the Templars along with a list of grand masters of the Temple.

1995 Interviewed in December for a possible TV documentary on the Sphinx, Egyptian Director of Antiquities Dr. Zahi Hawass discusses a yet to be explored tunnel under the Sphinx. Perhaps because of the public's intense interest in these ancient mysteries, Templar and Egyptian artifacts are often linked.

Professor Malcolm Barber writes Crusaders and Heretics, Twelfth to Fourteenth Centuries.

Reverend Lionel and Patricia Fanthorpe write <u>The Oak Island Mystery: The Secret of the World's Greatest Treasure Hunt</u>, a further investigation of the "money pit" on Oak Island.

1996 Christopher Knight and Robert Lomas publish two books on the Templars and Freemasonry in rapid succession -- <u>The Second Messiah: Templars, The Turin Shroud and the Great Secret of Freemasonry</u> and <u>The Hiram Key: Pharaohs, Freemasons, and the Discovery of the Secret Scrolls of Jesus</u>.

Richard Andrews and Paul Schellenberger publish the <u>Tomb of God: Body of Jesus and the Solution to a 2000 Year Old Mystery</u>, claiming the body of Jesus is buried under a mountain (Pech Cardou) near Rennes-le-Château. They calculate its location from decoding a complex system of geometry contained within the Saunière scrolls and paintings Saunière was especially interested in.

Shortly after publication of <u>Tomb of God</u>, BBC2's documentary series <u>Timewatch</u> produces <u>The History of a Mystery</u>, where Jean-Luc Chaumeil, a former associate of Pierre Plantard (1920-2000), reveals the story of the scrolls were fakes dreamed up by the Marquis Philippe de Chérisey and Plantard around 1957. Later, according to Chaumeil, these two fed the story to Gerard de Sède who then wrote about Rennes-le-Château in the 1960's.

In October, Christopher Knight and Robert Lomas arrange for Dr. Jack Miller, a Cambridge geologist, and Dr. Fernando Neves of the Colorado School of Mines to lead non-invasive ground scans around Rosslyn Chapel. They back out when the Rosslyn Chapel Trust requires "prior signature to a confidentiality agreement which would acknowledge the Trust's ownership of all intellectual property and other information which accrued in consequence of the investigation, including the fact that any investigation had taken place at all."

Chevalier Laurence Gardner publishes <u>Bloodline of the Holy Grail</u>, an extensive investigation of the existence and continuation of the Jesus bloodline using genealogical sources and the controversial work of Dr. Barbara Thiering.

1997 In March, The Rosslyn Chapel Trust constructs a steel shell around Rosslyn Chapel to dry the stonework and allow extensive repairs to begin.

In summer, The Friends of Rosslyn take over The Parsonage, a large house on the left side of the road leading to Rosslyn Chapel. The building will contain a Sinclair Library, a Templar Museum, the Roslin Heritage Museum, a Research & Study Center, a Gift Shop and Tea Room.

According to author Philip Coppen's website, http://www.philipcoppens.com/rosslyn_art1.html, Niven Sinclair and others perform their own unauthorized excavations at Rosslyn Chapel until Historic Scotland steps in. They find a tunnel leading from the chapel to the castle.

Lynn Picknett and Clive Prince publish <u>The Templar Revelation: Secret Guardians of the True Nature of Christ</u>. They determine, among many conclusions, that the Shroud of Turin is a five hundred year old "photograph" of Leonardo Da Vinci; that the highest secrets within the Templars and the Masons were Egyptian sacred sex practices leading to states of divine consciousness; that John the Baptist was a magician whose ministry was based on Egyptian Goddess rituals; and that Jesus stole these rituals from John the Baptist's movement.

Michael Baigent and Richard Leigh publish <u>The Elixir and the Stone</u>, a history of magic, alchemy, and Hermetic thought over the centuries. Meanwhile, their former partner Henry Lincoln recounts the tale of his <u>Holy Blood Holy Grail</u> investigation in <u>Key to the Sacred Pattern: The Untold Story of Rennes-le-Château</u>.

Charles G. Addison writes <u>The History of the Knights Templar</u> based on an 1842 account by a member of the "Inner Temple."

Mark Finnan writes <u>Oak Island Secrets</u>.

1998 Dr. Keith Laidler publishes <u>The Head of God</u> and concludes the head of Jesus, retrieved by Templars in Jerusalem, is buried in the crypt of Rosslyn Chapel below the famous Apprentice Pillar.

Martha G. E. H. Neyman publishes <u>The Horse of God: Et in Arcadia Ego</u> on CDROM, an extensive inquiry into the symbolism of Boudet's book and Languedoc geography. Neyman concludes the Ark of the Covenant is buried beneath the eastern tower of the Castle at Rennes-le-Château.

On April 2, H.R.H. Prince Charles officially opens a new visitor center at Rosslyn Chapel.

In June, Clan Gunn and Clan Sinclair hold a joint 600-year commemoration of Prince Henry Sinclair's landing in North America.

Professor Anne Gilmour-Bryson writes <u>The Trial of the Templars in Cyprus</u>, on the charges and proceedings against the Templars in Cyprus.

William Crooker publishes <u>Tracking Treasure</u>.

Andrew Sinclair writes <u>Discovery of the Grail</u>.

Robert Funk publishes <u>The Acts of Jesus: The Search for the Authentic Deeds of Jesus</u>, a follow up to <u>The Five Gospels</u> on The Jesus Seminar's conclusions about what Jesus really did and did not do.

Alan Butler and Stephen Dafoe, creators of http://www.templarhistory.org, publish <u>The Warriors and the Bankers: A History of the Knights Templar from 1307 to the Present</u>.

William F. Mann reveals in <u>The Labyrinth and the Grail</u> what he believes to be evidence of a Templar settlement in Nova Scotia created by Prince Henry Sinclair's voyage in 1399 from the Orkney Islands to North America.

Professor George Wells writes <u>The Jesus Myth</u>.

1999   Tim Wallace-Murphy and Marilyn Hopkins write in <u>Rosslyn: Guardians of the Secret of the Holy Grail</u> that a "leading American University will undertake ground scans of the vaults of Rosslyn Chapel and also examine the walls of the building."

In May, Stuart Beattie, Manager of the Rosslyn Chapel Trust, assures me in a personal interview there is no such permission to do any scanning or excavations.

Piers Paul Read writes <u>The Templars</u>, a history of the Knights and the Crusades.

Haft, White, and White write <u>The Key to the Name of the Rose</u>, a guide to medieval references used in Umberto Eco's famous novel.

Richard Andrews (sans Schellenberger) writes <u>Blood on the Mountain: A History of the Temple Mount from the Ark to the Third Millennium</u>,

Steven Sora writes <u>The Lost Treasure of the Knights Templar</u>, more about the Templars burying something important on Oak Island.

Douglas Lockhart publishes <u>The Dark Side of God: A Quest for the Lost Heart of Christianity</u>.

Laurence Gardner writes <u>Genesis of the Grail Kings: The Pendragon Legacy of Adam and Eve</u>.

2000   In January, yachtswoman Laura Zolo sails from Venice to the Orkney Islands to Nova Scotia, tracing the medieval routes of Nicolo Zeno and Prince Henry Sinclair.

Pierre Plantard, named by Baigent, Lincoln, and Leigh as a leader of the Prieuré de Sion, dies in February.

Earl Doherty, student of Professor George Wells, writes The Jesus Puzzle claiming Jesus never lived and that New Testament authors (writing many years after the death of Jesus) backdated his life so there wouldn't be any live witnesses to say otherwise.

Henry Lincoln and Erling Haagensen publish The Templar's Secret Island about the geography of Rennes-le-Château and Bornholm.

Release of The Knights Templar on videotape, narrated by Professor Malcolm Barber, who also publishes The Cathars: Dualist Heretics in Languedoc in the High Middle Ages.

On September 8th, Laura Zolo arrives at Guysborough Harbour in Nova Scotia.

Guy Patton and Robin Mackness write Web of Gold: The Secret Power of a Sacred Treasure linking Rennes-le-Château with all sorts of right-wing conspiracies.

Tim Wallace-Murphy and others publish Rex Deus: The True Mystery of Rennes-le-Château.

Professor Nicolas Haimovici Hastier publishes an extensive multi-lingual Templar bibliography, The Rule of the Order of the Templars.

2001   Karen Ralls, Oxford-based medieval historian and Celtic scholar, publishes <u>The Quest for the Celtic Key</u>, exploring many Scotland-related topics including the Knights Templar. Her database of Templar sites is at www.templarsites.org.uk.

Andrew Sinclair publishes <u>The Secret Scroll</u>, about how the Templars came to Scotland with their treasure and secrets after persecution in 1312. He explores the connection between the Templars, the Holy Grail, Rosslyn Chapel, the Sinclair family, and a scroll that is a "plan" of the Chapel found in the Kirkwall Masonic Lodge on the Orkney Islands.

Patrick Byrne writes <u>Templar Gold</u>, speculating Templars moved the Ark of the Covenant to Cyprus in 1307, later moving it to Pech Cardou in France until 1914, when it was moved again to the United States.

In April, researchers from the Merril Foundation conduct ground scans around the Tour Magdala at Rennes-le-Château, finding evidence of a chest buried around 12 feet beneath the floor. Plans are made for an excavation in September but it is pushed back until 2002. To date, no excavation is known to have taken place.

Vatican School of Paleontology professor Dr. Barbara Frale writes <u>The Last Battle of the Templars</u> asserting that Templar rituals underpinning the accusations against them were in fact hazing activities practiced by this all-male order.

James Wasserman writes <u>The Templars and the Assassins: The Militia of Heaven</u> about the connection between the famous knights and the famous killer cult.

Charing Cross Productions produces <u>The Prince and the Grail</u> on video.

2002	In March, Dr. Barbara Frale announces the discovery of the "Chinon Parchment," a scroll from the Vatican archives showing that Templar leaders who were burned at the stake had been exonerated of charges against them by Pope Clement V at Chinon nearly six years before.
	Graham Harris writes <u>Oak Island and Its Lost Treasure</u>.
	In October, Rosslyn Chapel offers an online prayer service, the first in Scotland.
	Mark Finnan writes <u>The Sinclair Saga: Exploring the Facts and the Legend of Prince Henry Sinclair.</u>
2003	In January, John Ritchie, Grand Herald and spokesman for the Militia Templi Scotia, starts sophisticated ground scans around Rosslyn Chapel. "The machine we are using is the most sophisticated anywhere and is capable of taking readings from the ground up to a mile deep without disturbing any of the land," says Ritchie at http://www.templarhistory.com.
	In March, Dan Brown writes <u>The Da Vinci Code,</u> a fast-paced mystery novel based on the idea of a bloodline descended from Jesus and Mary Magdalene. Publishers Weekly describes it as "an exhaustively researched page-turner about secret religious societies, ancient cover-ups and savage vengeance." It is an immediate bestseller.
	In June, Columbia Pictures buys the movie rights to the <u>Da Vinci Code.</u>
	John Young writes <u>Sacred Sites of the Knights Templar: Ancient Astronomer and Freemasons at Stonehenge, Rennes-Le-Chateau, and Santiago De Compostela</u> about European monuments and the meaning behind their placement and geography.

David Hatcher Childress publishes <u>Pirates and the Lost Templar Fleet: The Secret Naval War Between the Knights Templar and the Vatican</u>.

In October, Ron Howard, Brian Grazer and screenwriter Akiva Goldsman, the Oscar-winning trio from the movie <u>A Beautiful Mind</u>, announce they will film <u>Da Vinci Code</u> for Columbia Pictures for release in 2005.

Frank Sanello writes <u>The Knights Templars: God's Warriors, The Devil's Bankers</u>, a traditional history.

On November 8th, author Henry Lincoln receives an Honorary Knighthood in the Militi Templi Scotia order at Newbattle Abbey in Scotland.

In November, sparked by the popularity of <u>Da Vinci Code</u>, Elizabeth Vargas of ABC News hosts an hour-long special called <u>Jesus, Mary, and Da Vinci</u>, interviewing Dan Brown, Niven Sinclair, Andrew Sinclair, and others.

Gordon Napier writes <u>The Rise and Fall of the Knights Templar: The Order of the Temple, 1118-1314, True History of Faith, Glory, Betrayal and Tragedy.</u>

"We know many of the Knights are buried in the grounds and there are many references to buried vaults, which we hope this project will finally uncover." Karen Ralls writes in her book, <u>Knights of the Quest: The Templars & the Grail</u>.

2004   In March 2004, <u>Apprentice</u> and <u>Survivor</u> producer Mark Burnett buys film rights to Lewis Perdue's <u>The Da Vinci Legacy</u> and <u>Daughter of God</u>, novels with similar themes to Dan Brown's <u>Da Vinci Code</u> but written 20 years earlier.

In April, Rosslyn Chapel begins a £4 million preservation program, including a new visitor's center. Stuart Beattie says improvements are expected to be complete by 2008.

William Mann writes <u>The Knights Templar in the New World: How Henry Sinclair Brought the Grail to Acadia</u>.

Journalist Dan Burstein compiles <u>Secrets of the Code: The Unauthorized Guide to the Secrets Behind the Da Vinci Code</u>, a series of essays by those generally supporting the veracity of Dan Brown's sources. Several of the essayists are Dan Brown's sources. There's also <u>De-Coding Da Vinci: The Facts Behind the Fiction of The Da Vinci Code</u> by noted web blogger Amy Welborn. Refutations critical of <u>The Da Vinci Code's</u> basic premises include <u>The Truth Behind the Da Vinci Code: A Challenging Response to the Bestselling Novel</u> by Richard Abanes; <u>The Da Vinci Deception</u> by Erwin Lutzer; <u>Fact and Fiction in The Da Vinci Code</u> by Steve Kellmeyer; <u>The Da Vinci Hoax</u> by Sandra Miesel and Carl Olsen; <u>The Gospel Code</u> by Ben Witherington III; <u>Breaking the Da Vinci Code</u> by Darrell Bock; <u>Cracking Da Vinci's Code</u> by James Garlow and Peter Jones.

By this summer, according to Forbes, <u>Da Vinci Code</u> has sold $210 million in hardcover, $60 million in back listed Dan Brown novels, $10 million in audio books and an upcoming illustrated collection, and $75 million in paperbacks. With an upcoming movie and other spin-offs, <u>Da Vinci Code</u> "industry" could easily total over $1 billion.

In June, in the wake of renewed interest in his books from the success of <u>Da Vinci Code</u>, Michael Baigent signs a deal with Bluebook Films to produce a television series tentatively called <u>Revelation</u>.

Professor George Wells writes <u>Can We Trust the New Testament?: Thoughts on the Reliability of Early Christian Testimony</u>.

Phillip Coppens writes <u>The Stone Puzzle of Rosslyn Chapel: The Truth behind its Templar and Masonic secrets</u>.

Graham Phillips publishes <u>The Templars and the Ark of the Covenant: The Discovery of the Treasure of Solomon</u>, claiming that Templars once had the Ark of the Covenant and hid it in England.

In October, Variety reports that scenes for the upcoming <u>Da Vinci Code</u> movie will not be filmed at the Louvre, due to French policy regarding museum use. Rosslyn Chapel, however, says it will allow filming of the book's ending scenes on its grounds. Also this month, Baigent and Leigh consider suing Dan Brown, saying he "lifted the whole architecture" of the research they carried out with Henry Lincoln for <u>Holy Blood, Holy Grail</u>. According to the <u>New York Sun,</u> author Lewis Perdue is considering similar litigation.

Due in November: <u>Templars in America: From the Crusades to the New World</u> by Tim Wallace-Murphy and Marilyn Hopkins, founders of the European Templar Heritage Research Network.

2019 On July 28, according to author Tim Wallace-Murphy, the seven major planets will align with the locations of Rosslyn Chapel and the cathedrals at Amiens, Paris, Chartres, Orleans, Toulouse, and Compostela. This moment could be the apocalyptic creation of a new Jerusalem, he states, according to the <u>Bible's</u> Revelation of St. John. "Not a destruction of the world," Tim assures us, "but a transformation to a heaven on earth."

About The Author

When George Smart is not researching 12th century knights, he is Managing Partner of Strategic Development, Inc. in Research Triangle Park, North Carolina, USA. With 23 years experience in nearly 400 organizations such as IBM, Cisco, Microsoft, Boeing, Harvard Business School, and Bayer, George specializes in leadership for teams and executives. He is a frequent speaker to corporate leadership development programs and was 2004 Member of the Year for the Carolinas Chapter, National Speakers Association.

Printed in the United States
68228LVS00010B/16